Library of
Davidson College

*Archaeological Excavations in Southern Greece*

# Archaeological Excavations
# in Southern Greece

by
DOROTHY LEEKLEY
ROBERT NOYES

## NOYES PRESS
### PARK RIDGE, NEW JERSEY

Copyright © 1976 by Dorothy Leekley
   and Robert Noyes
Library of Congress Catalog Card Number: 76-17378
ISBN: 0-8155-5048-0

Published in the United States by
NOYES PRESS
Noyes Building
Park Ridge, New Jersey 07656

938
L485a

Library of Congress Cataloging in Publication Data

Leekley, Dorothy.
   Archaeological excavations in southern Greece.

   Bibliography: p.
   Includes index.
   1. Greece—Antiquities.  2. Excavations (Archaeology)—
Greece.  I. Noyes, Robert, joint author.  II. Title.
DF77.L37          938          76-17378
ISBN 0-8155-5048-0

77-4636

# FOREWORD

This book describes archaeological excavations undertaken in Southern Greece, including both Attica and the Peloponnese. It is the second of a series of three books which will relate to archaeological excavations in all of Greece. The previous volume, published in 1976, was entitled *Archaeological Excavations in the Greek Islands* and the forthcoming book will be entitled *Archaeological Excavations in Central and Northern Greece.*

The information given for each site in each of these volumes will include the names of excavators, the dates in which the excavations were carried out, a very brief description of the finds, and, most important, a bibliography which will enable the researcher to locate the book and/or article which describes in greater detail the excavations and finds in which he is interested. Reports of travelers and secondary literature are for the most part not included in this book.

Maps of the archaeological sites will not be included here. Current Greek maps are a hazardous trap for the unwary, and the authors have found that the drawing of maps and the precise locating of all these excavations on the maps are tasks which would require so much time as to delay the publication of the first three volumes. Plans to publish a fourth volume consisting solely of maps of the Greek archaeological sites are under way.

One of the reasons for publishing these books is to correct the present difficulty which exists in obtaining information on minor archaeological sites. Information on major excavations is simple enough to locate; consequently entries on such sites as Athens or Mycenae are very brief. This book contains information on all excavated sites in Southern Greece many of which can be considered as minor. For the most part, entries have been limited to sites at which planned excavations have taken place. Chance finds and rescue operations, except for the most important, have been excluded. These finds have been reported, since 1960, for all of Greece in *Archaeologikon Deltion.* Sites on which ancient remains have been noted, but not excavated, have also generally been omitted. Sites dating from all periods up to the Roman have been included, except for early Christian remains.

The information in this book is as current as possible up to the mid-1970s. However, it must be realized that many excavations of the Greek Archaeological Service are not reported for a few years after the work has been done. Those who use this book should utilize it in conjunction with the invaluable *Archaeological Reports* issued annually by the Council of the Society for the Promotion of Hellenic Studies and the Managing Committee of the British School at Athens as a supplement to *Journal of Hellenic Studies,* and the annual report published in *Bulletin de Correspondance Hellénique* issued by École française d'Athénes.

In every book of this nature, a question arises regarding the difficult task of transliterating Greek into English. The authors have used a "mixed" system, conforming to no particular rules, but attempting to choose the most commonly accepted spelling; historic spellings are used for the better known sites. The material presented in this book was taken from numerous periodicals in many languages, and no attempt has been made to transliterate any specific name on a consistent basis.

The sites in this book are organized by modern political nome, which vary somewhat from ancient political subdivisions. An index of all sites included in this book will be found at the end of the volume.

Miss Dorothy Leekley received her B.A. in Classics from Queens University, Kingston, Ontario, and is presently a doctoral student in Greek at Bedford College, University of London, working specifically on religion in Phyrgia in the Greek and Roman periods. Robert Noyes is a publisher of books relating to archaeology, classics and ancient history. He has been to Greece a number of times to visit sites, and is particularly interested in the relationship of Greek geography and prehistory.

# CONTENTS

## Attica

## Achaia

## Arcadia

## Argolid

## Corinthia

## Elis

## Laconia

## Messenia

# Attica

**ACHARNAI:** South of Acharnai (previously Menidi) at the place known as Lykotrypa, H. G. Lolling and the German School excavated a rich Mycenaean tholos tomb in 1879. (H. G. Lolling et al., *Das Kuppelgrab bei Menidi*, Deutsches Archaeologisches Institut, Athens, 1880). The pottery is LM IIIB except for some possibly LH IIIA2. There was some evidence for later cult in the dromos, where Archaic and Classical pottery was found (P. Wolters, *Jahrbuch*, 1898, 13ff; 1899, 103ff) (cf. *Gazetteer* no. 380) (cf. Ålin 111). Across the valley, one km southeast of the tholos, Hope Simpson noted traces of a settlement probably connected with the tomb. In addition to LH III sherds, Neolithic, possibly EH, and Classical sherds were noted (*BSA* 53-54, 1958–59, 292ff) (*Gazetteer* no. 381).

In 1959 at Ano Limni Zophra a sanctuary of an eranos dedicated to Herakles was found. A number of reliefs and inscriptions with lists of members of the eranos were recovered (*BCH* 1960, 655ff).

**AIGOSTHENA (Megarid):** The site of Aigosthena has been little explored. A series of terracotta figurines, and Geometric to Classical pottery have been found. There are remains of a Roman villa, overlying a cemetery. The fortifications are among the best preserved in Greece. The site has been described by E. F. Benson ("Aegosthena," *JHS* 15, 1895, 314ff) (cf. Highbarger 28f), R. L. Scranton (*Greek Walls*, 1941, 81) and F. E. Winter (*Greek Fortifications*, 1971, 142, note 56, and 145). Orlandos and Stikas excavated an early Christian basilica in 1954 (*PAE* 1954, 129ff) (cf. *AGC* 14, App. 2, 4-5).

**AMPHIAREION:** The site of ancient Oropos (at Skala Oropou) has not been excavated; attention has focused on the site of the Sanctuary of Amphiaraos, between Skala Oropou and Kalamos. The remains include a 4th century temple, a Hellenistic stoa, a theatre, baths, and accomodation for the pilgrims and patients. Excavation was begun in 1884 by Sp. Phintikles, B. Leonardos and W. Dörpfeld. Excavations continued, with a few breaks, until Leonardos' death in 1929 (Reports include: *PAE* 1884, 88ff; 1886, 51ff; 1887, 59ff; 1890, 31ff; 1904, 27f; 1906, 83ff; 1907, 119ff; 1913, 113ff; 1916, 65ff; 1927, 27ff; 1928, 41ff; 1929, 57ff) (*AE* 1922, 101ff; 1923, 36ff). The inscriptions discovered have been published in *AE* (*AE* 1884, 121ff through *AE* 1925–26, 9ff). I. Papadimitriou has done some cleaning on the site (*Ergon* 1957, 105f; 1958, 181f; 1960, 220f). (Cf. Bas. Petrakos, *O Oropos kai to ieron tou Amphiaraou*, Athens, 1968 for both the sanctuary and the city of Oropos.) (On the theatre: E. Fiechter, *Das Theater in Oropos, Antike Griechische Theaterbauten* Heft 1, Stuttgart 1930; and O.A.W. Dilke, *BSA* 45, 1950, 32ff.) (On the stoa: Ph. Versakis, *AM* 23, 1908, 247ff. Restudied by J. J. Coulter, *BSA* 63, 1968, 147ff.)

**ANAVYSSOS:** The bay of Anavyssos, in southwest Attica, was the center of the ancient deme of Anaphlyston. In 1911 Kastriotis and Philadelpheus excavated tombs of the Geometric period in a tumulus near the Ayios Georgios chapel south of modern Anavyssos village. The pottery dates to between 725–675. Near the village of Phokaia on the east side of the bay, 5th century sarcophagi have been found (*AD* 16, 1960, *Chr.* 39) (*AJA* 1961, 300). Other remains in the vicinity have been described (see A. Milchhöfer III, 20ff and Eliot 75ff, esp. 104ff). Middle Helladic sherds and apsidal buildings have been noted on the Ayios Nikolaos promontory; remains of walls, and Hellenistic and Roman sherds near the site of the 1911 excavations; and a settlement site by Ayios Pendeleimon north of the village.

In 1974, Mastrokostas described trial excavations where three Archaic funerary sculptures were found (*AAA* 7, 1974, 215ff).

**APHIDNAI:** The Kotroni acropolis at the northwest end of Lake Marathon has been identified with the ancient deme of Aphidnai. The site was occupied throughout antiquity. In 1894 S. Wide excavated MH graves in a tumulus near the acropolis in addition to investigating the acropolis itself (*AM* 1896, 385ff). MH, LH II–IIIB sherds have been noted on the acropolis (*Gazetteer* no. 380), as well as remains of later periods, and fortification walls whose date is not determined. Remains from the area of Aphidnai have been described by Princesses Sophia and Eirene, with Mrs. Th. Arvanitopoulou (*Ostraka ek Dekeleias*, Athens, 1959) and Mrs. Arvanitopoulou ("Dekeleia," *Polemon* 1958, parartima) (cf. *Hesperia* Suppl. XI, 81ff).

**ATHENS:** Archaeological activity in Athens has been intense and almost continuous since its liberation from the Turks in 1833. The amount of published material on Athens, both general and on specific excavations, is enormous, and much information is generally available. All that will be offered here is a survey of general areas of excavation and a bibliography which is far from complete, but is intended as a guide to where further information on excavations can be obtained.

Useful for information on early travellers, older bibliography, and general surveys of ancient Athens are:

W. M. Leake, *The Topography of Athens,* London 1841.

J. Stuart and N. Revett, *The Antiquities of Athens I–IV,* London 1762–1816.

L. Ross, *Archäologische Aufsätze* I–II, Leipzig 1855–1861.

J. G. Frazer, *Pausanias's Description of Greece,* vol. II, London 1898.

J. E. Harrison and M. de G. Verrall, *Mythology and Monuments of Ancient Athens,* London 1890.

J. E. Harrison, *Primitive Athens as Described by Thucydides,* Cambridge 1906.

W. Judeich, *Topographie von Athen,* 2nd ed., Munich 1931. Handbuch der klassischen Altertumswissenschaft III.2 (probably fullest bibliography for excavations up to 1931; hereafter Judeich).

For more recent bibliography:

I. T. Hill, *The Ancient City of Athens,* London 1953 (hereafter Hill).

J. Travlos, *Poleodomiki Exelixis ton Athinon,* Athens 1960 (hereafter Travlos, *Poleodomiki Exelixis*).

J. Travlos, *Pictorial Dictionary of Ancient Athens,* London 1971 (hereafter Travlos, *Dictionary*).

J. Travlos, *Athens, Ekistic Elements, First Report, Ancient Greek Cities* no. 17, Athens Center of Ekistics, Athens 1972; in modern Greek.

For Roman Athens, the series of books by Paul Graindor:

*Athènes sous Auguste,* Cairo 1927.

*Un milliardaire antique, Hérode Atticus et sa famille,* Cairo 1930.

*Athènes de Tibère à Trajan,* Cairo 1931.

*Athènes sous Hadrien,* Cairo 1934.

Rescue operations in the city are not generally covered here. They are reported annually in *Archaiologikon Deltion* since 1960 and the more important in *BCH* and *AR*.

**I.** *The Acropolis:* The Acropolis itself has naturally attracted much of the attention of archaeologists. Early work was concerned with clearing away the Medieval and Turkish additions and restoring the ancient monuments. Ludwig Ross, who served as Ephor-General of Antiquities until 1836, was among those first concerned with the acropolis. One of the chief works in which he was involved was the reconstruction of the temple of Athena Nike. The temple had been pulled down in 1687 and the material used to build a fortification in front of the Propylaea (L. Ross, E. Schaubert, Chr. Hansen, *Der Tempel der Nike Apteros*, Berlin 1839). (For other work by Ross, see his *Archäologische Aufsätze*.) Mistakes in the reconstruction of the Nike temple and weakness of the foundation led to the temple being taken apart and rebuilt again between 1935 and 1940 by N. Balanos and A. Orlandos (N. Balanos, *AE* 1937, 776ff) (N. Balanos, *Les Monuments de l'Acropole; relèvement et conservation*, Paris 1939) (Orlandos, *BCH* 1947–48, 1ff) (Hill, 164ff) (Travlos, *Dictionary* 148ff).

In 1852 E. Beulé discovered the gate in front of the Propylaea, named the Beulé Gate after him. It was built c. 280 A.D. from material from the choregic monument of Nikias erected in 320/19 B.C. (E. Beulé, *L'Acropole d'Athènes*, I–II, Paris 1953–54).

Others carrying out investigation of the acropolis in these years included C. Bötticher (*Bericht über die Untersuchungen auf der Akropolis von Athen in Frühjahre 1862*, Berlin 1863).

Beginning in 1885 and through 1890 the major work of studying the acropolis and clearing it down to bedrock was carried out by P. Kavvadias with G. Kawerau and W. Dörpfeld, among others. It was initially planned to be directed by P. Eustratiadis and some work was carried out between 1882 and 1884 (*AE* 1883, 33ff). In the major excavation after 1885 the building periods of the various terraces and fortification walls were noted, and an enormous amount of sculpture and inscriptions were found. One of the more surprising discoveries was the foundations of a temple identified by Dörpfeld as the 'Old Athena Temple' (*AM* 1885, 275ff; 1886, 337f; 1887, 25ff, 190ff; 1888, 304ff; 1890, 420ff) (P. Cavvadias and G. Kawerau, *Die Ausgrabung der Akropolis vom Jahre 1885 bis zum Jahre 1890*, Athens 1906: text in parallel Greek and German, with summary of excavations on acropolis up to 1885 and from 1890 to the date of publication) (J. E. Harrison, *Primitive Athens*, Chapters 1 and 2 for summary of excavation and plans) (Hill, 135ff). For unpublished photographs and summary see J. A. Bundgaard (*The Excavation of the Athenian Acropolis 1882–90*, Copenhagen 1974).

Most of the reconstruction of the monuments on the acropolis was done in the period after this task of clearing. The major work of restoration on the Parthenon was begun in 1895 after the earthquake in 1894, and was directed by Balanos through 1933. The Erechtheum had been partially reconstructed by Pittakis, Ross's successor, between 1837 and 1840, and Bötticher had also worked on it (Bötticher, op. cit.). The major work of reconstruction was directed by Balanos between 1902 and 1908 (L. D. Caskey et al., *The Erechtheum*, Cambridge, Mass. 1927: major study of the Erecteum with summary of excavation 560ff). (For reconstruction of various monuments: N. Balanos, *Les Monuments de l'acropole; relèvement et conservation*, Paris 1939.)

On Mycenaean Athens, see among others:
   S. Iakovidis, *Mikinaiki Akropolis ton Athinon*, Athens 1962.
   C.-G. Styrenius, *Submycenaean Studies*, Lund 1967.
   N. C. Scoufopoulos, *Mycenaean Citadels, Studies in Mediterranean Archaeology* no. 22, Göteborg 1971, 69ff.
   V. R. d'A. Desborough, *The Last Mycenaeans and Their Successors*, Oxford, 1964.
   S. A. Immerwahr, *Agora XIII, The Neolithic and Bronze Ages*, 1971.
   M. A. Pantelidou, *Ai Proistorikai Athenai*, Athens 1975.

**II.** *The North Slopes of the Acropolis:* One of the earliest sites excavated on the north slopes of the acropolis was the Klepsydra spring, which had been in use throughout antiquity and most of the Medieval period. It was rediscovered and cleared by K. Pittakis in 1822 during the Greek occupation of the acropolis (*AE* 1853, 1066) and excavated by Émile Burnouf in 1874 (*La ville et l'Acropole d'Athènes*, Paris 1877) and by Kavvadias in 1897. It was completely excavated by the American School between 1937–40 (*Hesperia* 7, 1938, 332ff; 12, 1943, 191ff).

What was intended to be a systematic excavation of the north slopes (including the Klepsydra) was begun by the Greek Archaeological Society under Kavvadias in 1896. They excavated the cave sanctuaries beneath the walls and the Mycenaean stairway leading up to the acropolis from the Cave of Aglauros (*AE* 1897). Excavations were carried out on the north and northeast slopes by the American School under O. Broneer from 1931 to the beginning of the war. They identified various sanctuaries, including that of Aphrodite and Eros. Neolithic and Mycenaean pottery was found on the slopes (*Hesperia* 1, 1932, 31ff; , 1933, 329ff; 4, 1935, 123ff; 5, 1936, 247ff: cave on east slope; 6, 1937, 539ff: Neolithic pottery; 7, 1938, 161ff, 264ff; 9, 1940, 141ff). One of the more important discoveries was that the passage in the Cave of Aglauros led much further down to a spring in use in the second half of the 13th century B.C. (*Hesperia* 8, 1939, 317ff).

More recently investigation has been carried out on the north slopes to reconstruct the course of the ancient peripatos (*AD* 21, 1966, *Chr.* 1, 43ff; 25, 1970, *Chr.* 1, 25ff; 26, 1971, *Chr.* 1, 27ff) (*AAA* 3, 1970, 167ff).

**III.** *South Slopes:* The excavation of the Odeion of Herodes Atticus was directed by Pittakis in 1848–58 (*AE* 1858, 1707ff) and by I. Miliadis in 1955–59 when it was reconstructed (*PAE* 1955, 36ff; 1956, 262ff; 1957, 23ff; 1959, 5ff).

The Stoa of Eumenes was excavated by the Archaeological Society under S. Koumanoudis in 1877–88 (*PAE* 1877, 12ff) (cf. Dörpfeld, *AM* 1888, 100ff). A Neolithic tomb was discovered by Skias after rains (*AE* 1902, 123ff) and a Neolithic house was excavated in the area by the Italian School under Della Seta in 1922 and 1924 (*Ann.* 13–14, 1930–31, 411ff). Neolithic and Mycenaean material has been found in recent excavation (*AD* 20, 1965, *Chr.* 1, 22ff).

The area of the Asklepieion had been excavated by Koumanoudis in 1876–77 (*PAE* 1876, 14ff; 1877, 6ff) (cf. *AM* 1877, 171ff, 229ff) and more recently by Platon (*AD* 18, 1963, *Chr.* 1, 18ff).

Excavation of the Theatre of Dionysos began in 1838 and investigations have taken place at intervals ever since. The more important were those conducted by A. S. Rousopoulos and Strack in 1862 (*AE* 1862), by Dörpfeld between 1886 and 1895 (W. Dörpfeld and E. Reisch, *Das griechische Theater*, Athens 1896), by H. Bulle in 1923 (*Untersuchungen an griechische Theatern,*Munich 1928), an exhaustive examination by E. Fiechter in 1927–29 and 1933 (*Das Dionysos-Theater in Athen* I-III, Stuttgart 1935–36) (cf. A. W. Pickard-Cambridge, *The Theatre of Dionysos in Athens,* Oxford 1946), investigations in the area by J. Travlos in 1951 (*PAE* 1951, 41ff) (*AE* 1953–54, part 2, 301ff) and by P. Kalligas in 1961–62 (*AD* 18, 1963, *Chr.* 1, 12ff).

The remains of the Odeion of Pericles, adjoining the theatre, were excavated by P. Kastriotis between 1914 and 1927 (*AE* 1914, 141ff; 1915, 145ff; 1922, 25ff) (*AD* 5, 1919, *par.* 1ff) (*PAE* 1919 through 1927) and by A. Orlandos between 1928 and 1931 (*PAE* 1931, 25ff; 1932, 27f).

**IV.** *Area west of the Acropolis:* While the location of the Classical Agora was always known, the location of the older, pre-Solonian Agora is still a subject of controversey. Wilhelm Dörpfeld believed that it lay west of the Acropolis extending to the area between the Areopagos and the Pnyx, and that the Panathenaic Way passed from the later Agora to the west and south of the Areopagus (*Alt-Athen und seine Agora* I, 1937, 32ff). J. Travlos argues that it extended from the west slope around to the north to include the civic buildings there such as the Anakeion and the area of the Eleusinion (Travlos, *Poleodomiki Exelixis* 24ff). Oikonomides places it on the south slopes (Al. N. Oikonomides, *The Two Agoras in Ancient Athens*, Chicago 1964). The various views are summarized and discussed by R. E. Wycherley (*Phoenix* 20, 1966, 285ff).

Dörpfeld directed some excavations in the area between the Areopagus and the Pnyx beginning in 1892 which he believed confirmed his hypothesis. However, he uncovered few substantial remains—mostly house walls of various periods and cross streets leading up toward the Acropolis. He excavated two sanctuaries, one of the hero Amynos, and one which he identified, not very plausibly, as the sanctuary of Dionysos in the Marshes. He also found remains of a fountain house which he identified as the Enneakrounos Spring (*AM* 1892, 439ff; 1894, 143ff; 496ff; 1895, 161ff; 1896, 265ff; 287ff) (*AE* 1894, 1ff, in reply to Nikolaidis in *AE* 1893, 177ff) (*Alt-Athen* I, 88ff) (J. E. Harrison, *Primitive Athens*, Cambridge 1906, is largely a defence of Dörpfeld's views. On these excavations: 83ff, 111ff, and her bibliography, 160ff).

The location of the Enneakrounos Spring has been one of the more disputed points of Athenian topography. The remains found by Dörpfeld are now accepted as being part of the Peisistratean water system, and the Enneakrounos is perhaps one of the fountains more recently located in the later agora (*Hesperia* 22, 1953, 29ff) (cf. *Ann.* 23-24, 1961–62, 149ff).

On the Pnyx Hill there had been several small excavations in the semi-circular assembly area (*Papers of the Am. School,* 4, 1885–86, 207ff) and in 1910 excavations by the Greek Archaeological Society under Kourouniotis confirmed this identification of the site as the Pnyx or meeting place of the Athenian assembly (*PAE* 1910, 127ff; 1911, 100ff). Between 1930 and 1937 H. A. Thompson in collaboration with Kourouniotis and R.L. Scranton thoroughly excavated the Pnyx, the fortifications on the hill, and the 'diateichisma' wall which connected the Mouseion Hill, the Pnyx Hill and the Hill of the Nymphs (*Hesperia* 1, 1932, 90ff; 5, 1936, 151ff; 12, 1945, 269ff; *Hesperia* Suppl. VII, 1943; Suppl. X, 1956).

The Philopappos Monument on the Mouseion Hill, built c. 114–16 A.D., was excavated by Skias in 1898-99 (*PAE* 1898, 68ff; 1899, 18). Travlos and H. A. Thompson excavated briefly in 1940 (Travlos, *Poleodomiki Exelixis* 122ff) (cf. M. Santangelo, *Ann.* 3-5, 1941–43, 153ff).

**V.** *The Agora:* Excavations in the Agora had been planned ever since the liberation, but the area was almost completely covered with houses and only a few small excavations were carried out. The Stoa of Attalos, part of which had always remained visible, was excavated by the Greek Archaeological Society between 1859–62, and 1898–1902. It was identified by an inscription found in 1861 (*IG* II², 317) (cf. *PAE* 1898, 65ff; 1899, 70ff; 1900, 31ff; 1901, 31ff; 1902, 46) (Judeich, 354ff). The so-called Stoa of the Giants, part of the Odeion of Agrippa, was also excavated about this time (*PAE* 1858, 14ff; 1870, 12ff; 33ff). Dörpfeld directed some excavations on the west side of the Agora in 1896–97, searching for the Stoa Basileios (*AM* 1896, 107ff; 1897, 225) (*Alt-Athen* I-II, Berlin 1937–39). Judeich has written on pre-1931 excavations in the Agora as a whole (Judeich, 328ff).

After negotiations with the Greek government, major excavation on the Agora was begun in 1931 by the American School, and work has continued up until the present except during the war. The excavations were directed by Theodore Leslie Shear from 1931 to 1940, by H. A. Thompson from 1946 to 1967 and by T. L. Shear Jr. since 1968. The Agora has naturally enough been one of the most important areas of Athens to be excavated. The excavation of the Tholos or Prytanikon in 1933–34 and 1936–37 furnished a point from which other buildings in the Agora were gradually identified (*Hesperia* 4, 1935, 311ff; 470ff; *Hesperia* Suppl. IV, 1940). The Stoa of Attalos was completely excavated from 1949–53 and from 1953–56 was reconstructed as the Agora Museum (*Hesperia* 18 through 26, 1949–1957). Excavation tapered off during the late 1950s and early 60s, with work being concentrated on small probes, consolidation, and study. A new phase began in 1970 with the extension of the excavation to the north of the Piraeus-Athens Railway line, where the 6th century B.C. Stoa Basileios (previously identified with the Stoa of Zeus Eleutherios on the west side) was excavated. Work was also extended to the east of the Stoa of Attalos toward the Roman Agora (Reports in *Hesperia*, beginning with vol. 2, 1933; Final publication: *The Athenian Agora* I, 1953 through XX, 1971 and XV, 1974; *Hesperia* Supplements 1, 1937; 2, 1939; 4, 1940; 5, 1941; 6, 1941; 9, 1951. Agora *Picture Books* nos. 1-16, 1958–76. Also, *The Athenian Agora, A Guide to the Excavations and Museum*, 2nd edition, Athens 1962).

The Roman Agora, or the commercial section of the market, lay to the east of the Greek Agora. The monumental gate to the rectangular colonnade had remained visible, and Bötticher conducted a short excavation in 1862 (*Bericht über die Untersuchungen auf den Akropolis von Athen in Frühjahre 1862*, Berlin 1863). The Greek Archaeological Society under S. Koumanoudis carried out an excavation in 1890–91 (*PAE* 1890, 11ff; 1891, 7ff), and in 1910 under A. Philadelpheus (*PAE* 1910, 112ff). Ph. Stavropoulos excavated in 1931 (*AD* 13, 1930–31, *par.* 1ff) and Miss E. Zaganiari under Platon in 1965–66 (*AD* 20, 1965, *Chr.* 1, 34ff; 21, 1966, *Chr.* 1, 44f). The Library of Hadrian, built north of the Roman Agora in 132 A.D. was excavated by the Greek Archaeological Society in 1884–85 (*PAE* 1884, 22; 1885, 13ff) (*AE* 1888, 57ff). In 1969 G. Dontas cleared the remains and began to excavate the rest of the building (*AAA* 3, 1970, 170) (*AD* 25, 1970, *Mel.* 162ff; *Chr.* 1, 28ff; *AD* 26, 1971, *Chr.* 1, 29) (Judeich 370ff for the Roman Agora and Hadrian's Library).

**VI.** *Kerameikos and Dipylon:* Excavations in the area of the Diplyon and Sacred Gates and the Outer Kerameikos have been almost continuous since 1863, when the Greek Archaeological Society began work which they continued until 1913 (*PAE* for years 1872–75, 1879–1880, 1890). A. Brückner had begun work in the area in 1907 in collaboration with the Greek Archaeological Society, and the Germans took charge of the excavations in 1913 made possible with a grant from G. Oberländer. Excavations were later directed by K. Kübler. After W.W. II work was resumed by D. Ohly in 1956, and since 1962 had been directed by F. Willemsen. The gates and buildings around them, such as the Pompeion used for preparation for the Panathenaic procession were excavated, but it is the finds from the cemeteries outside the gates which have made the excavations famous. Sub-Mycenaean, proto-Geometric, Geometric, and Archaic cemeteries have been found, as well as graves of the Classical period. The enormous amphoras used as grave markers in the 8th century have given the name to 'Dipylon style' painting (preliminary reports in *AM* for years 1926–28, 1930, 1931, 1934) (*AA* 1930 through 1943) (*AA* 1964, 384ff: particularly on Dipylon Gate; *AA* 1965, 277ff: summary of Ohly's excavations 1956–61; *AA* 1969, 31ff: 1964–66 excavations) (*AM* 1966, 1ff; *AM* 1970: entire issue devoted to Kerameikos; *AM* 1974, 1ff) (*AD* 16, 1960, *Chr.* 19ff; 17, 1961–62, *Chr.* 16ff; 18, 1963, *Chr.* 1, 22ff; 19, 1964, *Chr.* 1, 38ff; 20, 1965, *Chr.* 1, 21, 1966, *Chr.* 1, 51ff; 23, 1968, *Chr.* 1, 24ff; 25, 1970, *Chr.* 1, 31ff ) (*AAA* 5, 1972, 258ff) (cf. G. Karo, *An Attic Cemetery,* Oberländer Trust, Philadelphia 1943, for summary of excavations) (cf. Hill, 23ff; 32ff) (Final publication: *Kerameikos* I-VI, 1939–70; see also: W. Hoepfner, *The Pompeion,* Kerameikos Book no. 1, Athens 1971; J. Frel, *Panathenaic Prize Amphoras,* Kerameikos Book no. 2, Athens 1973; I. Scheibler, *The Archaic Cemetery,* Kerameikos Book no. 3, Athens 1973).

**VII.** *The Academy:* The area of the Academy was partially excavated between 1929 and 1940 by P. Aristophron directed by K. Kourouniotis, and by the Greek Archaeological Society under Ph. Stavropoulos beginning in 1953. A gymnasium complex and a 4th century B.C. square peristyle have been excavated within the Academy precinct. To the west of the western precinct wall Neolithic, EH, and MH pottery was found. In 1955 an EH apsidal house was excavated, and a house of the Geometric period was uncovered nearby (*PAE* for years 1955–56, 1958, 1959, 1961, 1963). Since then, Miss O. Alexandri has reported smaller rescue operations in the vicinity, including the discovery of a boundary stone which fixed the northeast side of the precinct (*AAA* 1, 1968, 101ff) (*AD* 16, 1960, *Chr.* 33ff; 22, 1967, *Chr.* 1, 46ff; 59ff).

**VIII.** *Olympieion Area:* The Olympieion was excavated by F. Penrose in 1883–86 and by G. Welter in 1922 (*Papers of the Am. School* 1, 1882–83, 183ff) (*AM* 1922, 61ff; 1923, 182ff). The area in and around the temple has also been explored at various times by the Greek Archaeological Society (*PAE* 1886, 13ff; 1888, 15ff; 1897, 14f; 1898, 62ff; 1900, 29f; 1901, 29ff; 1949, 25ff) (Judeich, 382ff).

Since 1956 Travlos has been working in the area, particularly to the south of the Olympieion in the area of the Ilissos River (Travlos, *Dictionary*, 402ff, 289ff). The remains of many buildings were uncovered, but most of them cannot definitely be identified, though probable identifications are given by Travlos, among them: the Temple of Apollo Delphinios (*Pictorial* 83) (*AD* 17, 1961–62, *Chr.* 9ff); the Temple of Kronos and Rhea (*Pictorial* 335) (*AD* 17, 1961–62, *Chr.* 9) (cf. *PAE* 1893, 130ff); the Panhellenion (*Pictorial* 429ff) (*Hesperia* 32, 1963, 57ff); a Gymnasion, previously excavated by C. Smith in 1896–97 (*BSA* 1895–96, 22) (*AAA* 3, 1970, 6ff), and a stoa, perhaps the lawcourt at the Palladion (*Hesperia* 43, 1974, 500ff) (*Pictorial* 412ff).

The Stadium was excavated by E. Ziller in 1869–70. The reconstruction was supervised by A. Metaxas, subsidized by G. Averoff (E. Ziller, *Ausgrabungen um Panathenäischen Stadion*, Berlin 1870).

**AYIOS IOANNIS RENTIS (between Athens and Piraeus):** A fourth century tomb enclosure containing seven marble sarcophagi and two burials in marble lekythoi was reported (*AD* 18, 1963, *Chr.* 1, 47ff). P. Lazaridis reported on the discovery of an Archaic kore figure in 1967 (*AAA* 1, 1968, 34).

**AYIOS KOSMAS:** In 1930–31 and 1951 George E. Mylonas excavated a Bronze Age settlement on the Ayios Kosmas promontory near Helliniko, of which the EH remains are the most important. There were two phases of the EH settlement, the second of which was destroyed by fire at the beginning of the MH period; a few sherds of Minyan ware were found on the site, but it appears to have been unoccupied during the MH period. Remains of a settlement of LH II–LH IIIB or C were also found. Some intramural child burials were found in cist graves below LH III houses; also two larnax burials. The water level has risen and much LH material was on a submerged reef.

EH cemeteries were found on the shore both north and south of the neck of land connecting the promontory to the mainland. Part of the cemetery is under water. Thirty-two cist graves were excavated in the north cemetery and seven graves, all plundered, in the south cemetery.

Ayios Kosmas is probably the ancient Cape Kolias, where there had been a temple of Aphrodite Kolias and the sanctuary of Demeter and Kore where the Thesmophoria was celebrated. A few ancient worked blocks were found, but modern buildings and terracing on the north side of the headland have perhaps destroyed other remains. Classical and Hellenistic miniature vases have been recovered from the seabed here (Preliminary reports: *AJA* 1934, 258ff) (*AE* 1952, 117ff) (G. E. Mylonas, *Aghios Kosmas,* Princeton 1959) (cf. Desborough, 112) (*Gazetteer* no. 353) (Ålin 104-5).

**BRAURON:** In 1894 Stais excavated three Mycenaean chamber tombs at Brauron (*PAE* 1894, 20ff) (*AE* 1895, 196ff) but it was not until 1948 that major excavations were begun at the site by the Archaeological Society under I. Papadimitriou. The sanctuary of Artemis Brauronia, at the foot of the Ayios Georgios hill, has been excavated, including the temple, a stoa, which probably served as the residence of the girl priestesses, a cave-shrine of Iphigeneia, and an earlier temple. While some of the buildings go back to the 6th century, Geometric sherds and small votives were found in a pit. On the Ayios Georgios acropolis and its slopes house remains of MH period and LH I–IIIC have been found; also some EH material. The chamber tombs are located on the Chamolia ridge opposite the acropolis. I. Sakellaraki has also taken part in the excavation (*PAE* 1948, 81ff; 1949, 75ff; 1950, 188ff; 1956, 73ff; 1957, 42ff) (*Ergon* 1956, 28ff; 1957, 20ff; 1958, 30ff; 1959, 13ff; 1960, 21ff; 1961, 20ff; 1962, 25ff) (On relation of the buildings and cult: Kondis, *AD* 22, 1967, *Mel.* 156ff) (*Gazetteer* no. 368) (On the stoa: Kh. Boura, *Anastilosis tis stoas tis Brauronos*, Dimosieumata tou Arkhaiologikou Deltiou XI, Athens, 1967) (P. G. Themelis, *Brauron—Guide to the Site and Museum,* Athens, 1971).

**DAPHNI:** The Daphni monastery incorporates building material from a sanctuary of Apollo. About a mile along the Sacred Way to Eleusis from the Monastery is the sanctuary of Aphrodite and wall mentioned by

Pausanias (I.37.7). The sanctuary was partially excavated by D. Kampouroglous in 1892 *(AD* 1892, 4-5, 37f) (cf. S. Wide, *AE* 1910, 35ff). From 1936 to 1939 Travlos worked in the area, excavating the temple and associated buildings, and the peribolos wall which preceded the temple. In the cliff behind the temple are numerous niches for votives. Travlos also excavated 4th century graves surrounded by a peribolos wall and the section of the Sacred Way between the temple and the Reitoi (Limni Koumoudourou) *(PAE* 1936, 27ff; 1937, 25ff; 1938, 28ff; 1939, 39ff).

**DEKELEIA:** Princesses Sophia and Eirene with Mrs. Th. Arvanitopoulou have described antiquities from the area of Dekeleia (Tatoï) and Aphidnai *(Ostraka ek Dekeleias,* Athens, 1959) (Th. A. Arvanitopoulou, "Dekeleia," *Polemon* 1958, parartima) (cf. *Hesperia* Suppl. XI, 56ff for remains of fortifications and possible location of the Spartan camp at Dekeleia).

**DEMA WALL:** The 'Dema Wall' or 'Aigaleos-Parnes Wall' is an ancient fortification closing the gap between Mt. Parnes and Aigaleos. The nearest town is Ano Liosia. It has often been discussed and various dates have been assigned ranging from the 8th to 4th century B.C. (Milchhöfer, II, 44ff) (Skias, *AE* 1919, 35) (R. L. Scranton, *Greek Walls,* 1941, 39ff) (Sterling Dow, *Hesperia* 11, 1942, 193ff) (R. Martin, *BCH* 1947, 135ff). The wall, which is 4,360 meters long, was accurately surveyed by J. E. Jones, L. H. Sackett and C. W. J. Graham in 1955. They date the wall to the second half of the 4th century *(BSA* 52, 1957, 152ff including a full bibliography of earlier literature) (cf. *Hesperia* Suppl. XI. 63ff). They also noted a Classical farmhouse on the west side of the wall which they fully excavated in 1960. They date the house to the period of the Peace of Nikias *(BSA* 57, 1962, 75ff).

**DIONYSOS:** In 1887 the American School under Professor Merriam began excavations at Dionysos in the ancient deme of Ikaria, traditionally the first place in Attica visited by Dionysos. Excavations continued through 1888–89. A theatre, a shrine of Pythian Apollo, and the temenos wall of the sanctuary of Dionysos were excavated. Most of the remains date from the 4th century B.C. *(AJA* 4, 1888, 421ff; 5, 1889, 9ff) (On the theatre: O.A.W. Dilke, *BSA* 45, 1950, 30ff).

**ELEUSIS:** Systematic excavation of Eleusis began in 1882 and has continued with few breaks since. For a history of the site until then and a summary of the excavations, along with a discussion of the remains and of the Eleusinian religion, see G. E. Mylonas, *Eleusis and the Eleusinian Mysteries*, Princeton 1961. D. Philios, with the collaboration of W. Dörpfeld, excavated the main sanctuary from 1882–1893 (*PAE* 1882, 84ff and subsequent years through 1893) (Inscriptions and sculptural material: *AE* 1883, 110ff, 134ff, and subsequent years through 1890) (cf. *BCH* 1884, 254ff; 1885, 5ff). From 1894 to 1898 and in 1902 excavations were directed by Skias. The exploration of the sanctuary appeared to be complete and he turned his attention to the acropolis, where he excavated a necropolis with Mycenaean and Geometric tombs on the south slopes (*PAE* 1894, 14ff, and subsequent years through 1898; 1907, 47) (*AE* 1898, 29ff; 1895–97 excavations in necropolis; 1912, 1ff: 1898 and 1902 excavations).

K. Kouronouniotis became interested in the site and in 1930 with the aid of the Rockefeller Foundation began work with Mylonas, J. Travlos, I. Threpsiadis and G. Bakalakis. Work continued until 1940. An extensive prehistoric settlement was excavated—EH on the top of the acropolis; MH, LH and Geometric occupation on the south slopes. The sacred precinct was reexamined and remains of a Mycenaean building were found beneath the Telesterion, and a Mycenaean level beneath the Lesser Propylaea (*AD* 13, 1930–31, *par.* 17ff; 14, 1932, *par.* 41ff; 15, 1933–35, 54ff: summary of site; *AD* 15, 1933–35, *par.* 1ff: excavation) (*PAE* 1935, 71f; 1936, 34ff and subsequent years to 1940) (*AJA* 1932, 104ff; 1933, 271ff; 1936, 415ff) (G. E. Mylonas, *Proistoriki Eleusis*, Athens 1932).

In 1950 work was resumed by Travlos and continued with Mylonas and the collaboration of Washington University in St. Louis. Others taking part included I. Threpsiadis, I. Phokas and Mrs. M. Anagnostopoulou. Mylonas worked mainly in the cemeteries until 1956; Travlos in the sanctuary until 1957 and again in 1960–64. The cemetery lies by the Megara road. Tombs of MH to late Mycenaean, proto-Geometric, Geometric, and 5th century to Roman times were excavated (*PAE* 1950, 122ff; 1952, 53ff; 1953, 72ff and subsequent years to 1956; *PAE* 1960, 10ff and subsequent years to 1964) (*Ergon* 1954 to 1957, 1960 to 1964) (Summary of work in the sanctuary from 1950–60: *AD* 16, 1960, *Chr.* 43ff) (On the Anaktoron: *AE* 1951, 1ff) (cf. Mylonas, *Eleusis and the Eleusinian Mysteries*, Princeton 1961) (Ålin 112-30) (Desborough passim) (*Gazetteer* no. 386).

Miss O. Alexandri reported on the excavation of a section of the Sacred Way east of the sanctuary (*AAA* 2, 1969, 323ff) and on small excavations within modern Eleusis town (*AD* 22, 1967, *Chr.* 1, 122ff; 23, 1968, *Chr.* 1, 104ff; 24, 1969, *Chr.* 1, 76ff; 25, 1970, *Chr.* 1, 91ff).

**ERENEIA (Megarid):** The site of Ereneia is perhaps Kastro tou Ayiou Georgiou, 6.5 km west of Palaiochori. I. Sarris examined the fortifications and proposed this identification (*AE* 1910, 151ff) (cf. Highbarger 29-30) (*AGC* no. 14, App. 2, 5-6). It has also been suggested that the remains are of an Attic border fort, not of Megarian Ereneia (*Hesperia* Suppl. XI, 85ff).

**MT. GERANIA (Megarid):** Miss Y. Nicopoulou reported a necropolis 19.5 km west of Megara on the road to the springs in the Gerania Mountains. There were 69 burials of the 5th–4th centuries and a proto-Corinthian monolithic sarcophagus of the first quarter of the 7th century (*AAA* 2, 1969, 339ff) (*AD* 25, 1970, *Chr.* 1, 102ff).

**MT. HYMETTOS:** In 1923–24 the American School under Blegen excavated at a point half a mile north of the highest peak and found an enormous amount of votive pottery, some of it proto-Geometric, but largely Geometric and sub-Geometric. Much of it had dedicatory inscriptions. What is probably an altar, perhaps of Zeus Ombrios, and an apsidal structure were uncovered (*Art and Archaeology* 16, 1923, 207ff; 17, 1924, 285f) (*AJA* 28, 1924, 337; 38, 1934, 10ff; inscriptions). In 1939 Blegen and Young conducted a short excavation at the site and recovered much more pottery (*AJA* 44, 1940, 1ff).

In 1949 N. Kotzias excavated on the Prophitis Elias peak above Koropi and uncovered remains of a 5th century temple with a peribolos wall, which he identified as the temple of Apollo Proöpsios. He continued his excavation in 1950 and discovered another temple he identified as that of Zeus Ombrios. In a cave at the foot of Prophitis Elias he found Mycenaean, Geometric, and 6th–5th century sherds (*PAE* 1949, 51ff; 1950, 144ff) (*Gazetteer* no. 351) (M. K. Langdon, *A Sanctuary of Zeus on Mt. Hymetta, Hesperia* Suppl. XVI, 1976).

See also Koropi for the 'Kastro tou Christou'.

**KALAMAKI:** An LH III chamber tomb was discovered in Kalamaki, south of Palaion Phaleron, during the war (*AA* 1943, 303) (*Gazetteer* no. 350).

**KALLITHEA:** Five Geometric graves were discovered during construction work in 1963 and were reported by V. Kallipolitis (*AD* 19, 1964, *Chr.* 1, 65ff). E. K. Tsirivakos reported sculptural material from late Classical funerary monuments (*AAA* 1, 1968, 35ff; 108ff).

**KHALANDRI:** In this suburb northeast of Athens, occupying the site of ancient Phlya, a Roman tomb has long been known by the chapel of Panayia Marmariotissa. It was investigated by H. Möbius in 1924 and has been compared with the Roman tomb at Kiphisia (*AM* 1927, 189ff) (cf. *RE* Suppl. Band 10, 1965, 535ff).

**KIPHISIA:** In 1866 a tomb containing four Roman sarcophagi with reliefs was found in the main square of Kiphisia by Eustratiatis (*AZ* 1868, 35ff). Herodes Atticus is connected with this area by inscriptions (*IG* III, 1417ff) and the tomb has been attributed to his family. Möbius compared this tomb to the one at Khalandri (q.v.) (*AM* 1927, 195ff). A. Tschira re-examined the chamber in 1942 (*AA* 1948–49, 83ff).

S. Dragoumis had suggested as long ago as 1875 that the villa of Herodes Atticus lay near the Panayia tis Xidhou Church, about one km northwest of the square, and in 1961 sculptures, including busts of Herodes Atticus and his pupil Polydeukion were found near it. Petrakos investigated the site and found some walls (*AJA* 1961, 299ff) (*AD* 17, 1961–62, *Chr.* 1, 29f).

**KITSOS CAVE:** The Kitsos cave, northwest of Laurion, was discovered in 1966, and after soundings in 1968 and 1969, the French School under Nicole Lambert began a major excavation which has continued since as a joint French-Greek project with the cooperation of Miss O. Apostolopoulou. Others taking part have included C. Prost, C. Perlès, R. Treuil, P. Themelis and S. Pitihouti. Excavations were carried out at several sectors both inside and outside the cave and in nearby rock shelters. Stratigraphy is very complex. Generally, Neolithic material was found directly below the Classical stratum, though some Mycenaean pottery was identified in one sector in 1972. Neolithic finds have included incised pottery, bone material, and obsidian objects. Neolithic material from level 4 was dated to about 4000 B.C. A carbon 14 sample from level

5a, where seashells, a polished bone tool, and large animal bones, including bear, were found, was found to be about 40,000 years old.

Since 1972 the excavation has also served as a school of prehistoric archaeology (*BCH* 1971, 703ff; 1972, 817ff; 1973, 413ff; 1974, 723ff) (*AAA* 7, 1974, 8ff) (*AD* 26, 1971, *Chr.* 1, 42ff).

**KOROPI:** N. Kotzias excavated in 1950 on the acropolis Kastro tou Christou or Ayios Christos about 3 km west of Koropi toward Prophitis Elias in Hymettos. He found LH IIIA–B sherds and Cyclopean walls (*PAE* 1950, 165ff) (cf. *AM* 16, 1891, 220). Åström has also reported settlement remains and plundered LH II–IIIA chamber tombs on the northeast side (Ålin 106).

At Vourvatsi, about halfway between Koropi and Vari, Kyparissis excavated seven Mycenaean chamber tombs in a large but plundered cemetery. The finds date from LH IIIA–C1 (*AD* 11, 1927–28, 65f) (*BSA* 42, 1947, 7) (Desborough 112) (*Gazetteer* no. 359).

**LAURION:** For mining remains in the Laurion area; see:
    E. Ardaillon, *Les Mines du Laurion,* 1897.
    C. W. J. Eliot, *The Coastal Demes of Attica,* Toronto 1962, passim.
    R. J. Hopper, "The Attic Silver Mines in the Fourth Century B.C.," *BSA* 48, 1953, 200ff.
    R. J. Hopper, "The Laurion Mines: A Reconsideration," *BSA* 63, 1968, 293ff.

For ancient mining in general see:
    R. J. Forbes, *Metallurgy in Antiquity,* Leiden 1950.
    R. J. Forbes, *Studies in Ancient Technology,* VII-IX.

Finds in a mining area about 4 km south of modern Laurion town are reported, and 4th century B.C. methods of separating silver and lead are discussed in *Kathimerini,* April 15, 1962.

Themelis described ancient mine-working remains below Kamariza village above Laurion (*AD* 24, 1969, *Chr.* 1, 91f).

See also Thorikos.

**LIOPESI (renamed Paiania):** Poor Mycenaean graves were excavated by

Keramopoulos in 1915, but the finds are not known (*AA* 1916, 142) (Ålin 106) (*Gazetteer* no. 370).

**LOUTSA:** In 1956–57 I. Papadimitriou, assisted by O. Alexandri and B. Petrakos, excavated a temple of Artemis Tauropolos. Sixth to fifth century pottery was found (*Ergon* 1957, 124f) (*BCH* 1958, 678).

**MARATHON:** In 1884 Schliemann briefly excavated in the 'soros' or burial mound of the Athenians who fell at Marathon, but gave up due to bad weather (*Zeitschrift für Ethnologie* 1884, 85ff). Stais excavated in 1890–91 and confirmed the traditional identification of the mound. He found a layer of ash and bone and early 5th century black-figure lekythoi (*AD* 1890, 123ff; 1891, 67, 97) (*AM* 1893, 46ff).

G. Soteriadis excavated in the Marathon area at various times from 1925 to 1939. He located the probable site of the ancient deme of Marathon about 1.5 km from the soros near Vrana village. Acropolis walls, and Classical and Geometric sherds were found (cf. *Hesperia* Suppl. XI, 35). By the chapel of Ayios Demetrios at the north foot of Mt. Agriliki he located a sanctuary of 5th century date, perhaps earlier, probably the sanctuary of Heracles. In the plain about one km west of the soros he excavated the chamber of a Mycenaean tholos tomb, finding pottery and a Mycenaean gold cup. The tholos was apparently later used as a heroon. Nearby he excavated a Geometric cemetery and a cemetery of the 5th–3rd centuries (*PAE* 1932, 28ff: 1925–26 excavation; *PAE* 1933, 31ff: 1931 excavation; *PAE* 1934, 29ff; 1935, 84ff; 1939, 27ff).

Papadimitriou excavated in 1957–58 the Cave of Pan near the Ninoe spring about 3 km west of modern Marathon town, below the acropolis of ancient Oinoe. Evidence was found of the Neolithic, EH, MH, LH I–II and LH III periods. The cave was a place of cult, but was deserted from the end of the Bronze Age until the 5th century, the introduction of the cult of Pan at that time probably being connected with the story of his appearance before the battle of Marathon (*Ergon* 1958, 15ff) (Ålin 111) (*Gazetteer* no. 379).

Papadimitriou, with Stikas, also excavated the dromos of the tholos excavated by Soteriadis. The skeltons of two horses were found at the beginning of the dromos (*Ergon* 1958, 23ff) (*BCH* 1959, 583ff) (Ålin 110) (*Gazetteer* no. 377).

The 'mandra tis graias', an enclosure wall about 3300 m long, with a monumental gateway and inscriptions referring to Herodes Atticus and his wife Regilla has been investigated by Soteriadis among others, but never thoroughly excavated. Its purpose is unknown (*PAE* 1935, 149f) (cf. *Hesperia* Suppl. XI, 35ff for further bibliography).

In 1968 an Egyptian style statue was found where another had been found in 1843, 1.5 km south of the soros. The walls and monumental gate of an Egyptian style building, possibly built by Herodes Atticus, were excavated by Vavritsas (*AAA* 1, 1968, 230ff).

From 1970–72 S. Marinatos excavated several important sites. On the Plasi hill he investigated a peribolos of polygonal walling which had been thought to be Archaic, but MH remains were found within, including matt-painted and Minyan ware. EH, MH and Mycenaean settlement remains were excavated including a potter's kiln and MH tombs; Geometric and/or Archaic remains and an early Christian basilica were also found. At 'Tsepi Vrana' at the entrance to the Vrana valley about a mile north of Plasi, he excavated a large cemetery of EH cist graves. A few hundred meters up the valley opposite the Ayios Georgios chapel he investigated four stone tumuli, the largest with a diameter of 16.70 meters. The tumuli contained tombs, mostly of an early type of shaft-grave chamber. One had a horse buried in it. The tombs ranged in date from MH to late Mycenaean. A larger tumulus about 120 meters to the west was identified as the tomb of the Plataeans killed at Marathon. The graves in it were contemporary with the Athenian soros. Inscriptions were found at Valaria. (*Ergon* 1970, 5ff; 1971, 5ff; 1972, 5ff) (*PAE* 1970, 5ff, with map; 1972, 5ff) (*AAA* 3, 1970, 14ff, 63ff, 53ff).

In 1965 E. Vanderpool in collaboration with N. Verdelis excavated a Mediaeval tower by the chapel of the Panagia Mesosporitisia in the northern part of the Marathon plain. It is constructed of reused ancient blocks including an Ionic column. Vanderpool suggests this was a pillar monument erected as a trophy by the Athenians after the Battle of Marathon (*Hesperia* 35, 1966, 93ff; cf. 36, 1967, 108ff).

**MARKOPOULO (Mesogaias):** In 1894 Stais excavated 22 LH IIIA–C1 chamber tombs at 'Kopreza', 2 km southeast of the village (*AE* 1895, 210ff) and ten LH IIIB–C1 tombs at 'Ligori', east of Markopoulo about halfway to the coast (*AE* 1895, 202ff). This is possibly the same necropolis in which Kyparissis excavated a chamber tomb in 1927 (*AD* 11, 1927–28, par. 59f). LH IIIA–B chamber tombs were excavated by Theocharis at Lapoutsi (Ålin 107) (*Gazetteer* nos. 364, 365, 366).

In 1950 Papadimitriou found 5th century vases in a cemetery at Markopoulo (*BCH* 1951, 111). Papachristodoulou reported Geometric and Classical graves found within the village in 1971 and what are possibly two EH graves (*AAA* 4, 1971, 143ff) (*AD* 26, 1971, *Chr.* 1, 38ff).

Merenda, about 3 km southeast of Markopoulo, is the center of the ancient deme of Myrrhinous. In 1951, 1960 and 1961 Papadimitriou, first with Theocharis, then with Mrs. K. Oikonomopoulou-Ninou, excavated in a vast cemetery along the ancient road with burials from Geometric through Classical periods, and found remains of what was probably the temple of Artemis Kolainis (*Ergon* 1960, 30ff; 1961, 37f). D. Lazaridis excavated tombs of the Geometric to Hellenistic periods and a Classical farmhouse (*AAA* 1, 1968, 31ff). Vavritsas reported the discovery in 1968 of a further cemetery mostly with Geometric tombs, but with a few late Classical and Roman (*AD* 25, 1970, *Chr.* 1, 127ff). E. Mastrokostas reported the discovery of an Archaic kouros and kore buried within the Geometric cemetery (*AAA* 5, 1972, 298ff).

**MEGARA:** The modern town of Megara occupies the site of the ancient city. H. G. Lolling made some topographical studies (*AE* 1890, 55ff), and in 1889 D. Philios carried out excavations in the Megara area, at what he identified as the temple of Zeus Aphesios and the tomb of Telephanes (*PAE* 1889, 25f) (*AE* 1890, 21ff) (cf. *AGC* no. 14, App. 4 for a reappraisal of the evidence). In the city itself, R. Dëlbruck and K. G. Vollmöller excavated the Fountain of Theagenes in the center of the town (*AM* 1900, 23ff) and I. Meliadis found Roman tombs on the western side of the city.

I. Threpsiadis excavated in Megara several times between 1932 and 1936. In 1932–33 he excavated late 6th century tombs at 'Kamari' on the north side of the city, and made a small excavation on the Caria acropolis (*AE* 1933, 119ff). In 1934 Threpsiadis and Travlos excavated on the Acropolis of Alcathous the site of the 6th century temple of Athena which had previously been identified by K. Schefold and H. Johannes (*AA* 1934, 149f). Only cuttings for the foundation remain, though Archaic sherds were found (*PAE* 1934, 39ff). In 1936 Threpsiadis excavated part of a bath complex, and the cave of Marmouni below the Caria acropolis, which was probably a Roman sanctuary of Demeter. He also found MH sherds in the city (*PAE* 1936, 43ff).

In 1953 Papadimitriou and Theocharis excavated ancient cisterns, a mosaic, and Hellenistic tombs (*BCH* 1954, 112) and in 1954 Mastrokostas found part of an Archaic kouros (*BCH* 1955, 227). In 1957 Papadimitriou with D. Ohly cleared the Fountain of Theagenes (*BCH* 1958, 688ff) (*AD* 19, 1964, *Mel.* 37ff).

Miss O. Alexandri worked in the city between 1966 and 1969, investigating particularly the ancient city wall (*AAA* 3, 1970, 21ff). She also reported on other excavations within the city including Hellenistic tombs and Hellenistic and later buildings (*AD* 22, 1967, *Chr.* 1, 118f; 23, 1968, *Chr.* 1, 100ff; 24, 1969, *Chr.* 1, 81ff).

Miss Y. Nicopoulou reported on numerous excavations carried out in 1969, including part of the city wall, a Geometric burial, Classical graves and part of an ancient road (*AD* 25, 1970, *Chr.* 1, 100ff). She also reported cemeteries of Classical and post-Classical date outside the city, particularly on the road to Mt. Gerania (q.v.). EH, MH, LH I and LH III material has been found in the city and it was probably an important settlement in the Mycenaean period (Ålin 114) (*Gazetteer* no. 390). Mrs. A. Kalogeropoulou reported on a grave stele (*AAA* 7, 1974, 287ff).

The two ports of Megara, Nisaea and Minoa, were on the coast to the south near Pachi. Various locations have been proposed, centering mostly on the question whether or not Minoa was an island in ancient times. The Palaiokastro hill, with remains of a Medieval castle, is partially surrounded by a swamp, and was first identified as Minoa, and the hill of Ayios Georgios above Pachi as Nisaea, by Spratt (*Journal of the Geographical Society* 8, 1838, 205ff), followed by Lolling (*AM* 1880, 1ff), S. Casson (*BSA* 19, 1912–13, 70ff) and Hope Simpson (*Gazetteer* no. 391).

F. Bölte and G. Weicker reversed the identification, placing Nisaea at Palaiokastro (*AM* 1904, 79ff) (cf. Ålin 114). A. J. Beattie, while placing Nisaea at Ayios Georgios, identified Minoa with Cape Ticho to the east. This identification was followed by M. Sakellariou and N. Pharaklas (*AGC* no. 14, 56ff. and passim). In addition to Classical and later remains on the Palaiokastro hill, EH, MH, LH I–IIIB sherds have been noted (*AM* 1904, 95) (*BSA* 11, 1912–13, 70ff). Threpsiadis and Travlos excavated on the hill in 1934, finding MH sherds, and Geometric and Byzantine graves (*PAE* 1934, 50ff).


**MEGARID:** H. J. W. Tillyard described fortification towers in the central Megarid (*BSA* 12, 1905–6, 10ff) and N. G. L. Hammond described others and discussed the topography of the Megarid (*BSA* 49, 1954, 103ff). On Megara and the Megarid see:

M. Sakellariou and N. Pharaklas, *Megaris, Aigosthena, Ereneia,*
     *Ancient Greek Cities* no. 14, Athens Technological Organization,
     Athens Center of Ekistics, 1972.
E. L. Highbarger, *The History and Civilization of Ancient Megara,* John
     Hopkins University Studies in Archaeology no. 2, Baltimore 1927.

For individual sites, see entries under Aigosthena, Ereneia, Mt. Gerania, Megara, and Pagai.

**MOSCHATON:** After finding a relief similar to the Echelos relief (*AE* 1893, 109 and 129ff) Stais excavated in 1908 for the Archaeological Society within the long walls at Moschaton and identified the sanctuary, probably of the Nymphs, from which the reliefs came (*PAE* 1908, 63) (*AE* 1909, 239ff).

In 1916 seventy Archaic burials, mostly of children, were excavated by the Archaeological Society (*AR* 1911–12, 385).

In 1965 a section of the 'middle wall' constructed in 445 B.C. was located (*AD* 21, 1966, *Chr.* 1, 92ff).

I. Papachristodoulou investigated a small shrine and peribolos wall where a 4th century statue of Cybele had been found (*Ergon* 1973, 7ff). He has also published a fuller account including a general report on the cult of Cybele in Attica (*AE* 1973, 188ff) (*Ergon* 1974, 7ff).

**NEA IONIA:** In 1949 Papadimitriou carried out a short excavation of a grave enclosure of proto-Geometric date. Within the enclosure were four cremation burials in pithoi and associated pyres, as well as two cist graves of children. The pottery is dated to the late 10th century. LH IIIA–B sherds were noted in the vicinity (*BCH* 1949, 525) (Pottery published by E. L. Smithson, *Hesperia* 30, 1961, 147ff).

**NEA MAKRI:** In 1954 Theocharis investigated an extensive Neolithic settlement on the south edge of the Marathon plain (*PAE* 1954, 114ff) (*BCH* 1955, 225).

**PAGAI (Megarid):** The site of the ancient city of Pagai is near Alepokhori in the Megarid. A tower and rampart were noted and sherds of the Geometric and later periods (*AM* 1904, 99ff) (*AGC* no. 14, App. 2, 3-4) (cf. Highbarger 27-28).

**PALAION PHALERON:** On the shore at Voidolivadou K. Kourouniotis excavated in 1910 68 graves of which 44 were child burials in amphora. The pottery was Geometric (*AE* 1911, 241ff).

During the war the Germans dug a LH IIIA chamber tomb (*AA* 1943, 303) (Ålin 103-4).

**MT. PARNES:** In 1959 below the summit of the mountain Mastrokostas investigated a sacrificial pyre, perhaps an altar of Zeus, with a deposit over 2 meters deep. Over 3000 iron knives and Early Geometric–Archaic pottery were found. In a nearby cave Roman lamps were found. The location was not reported precisely (*BCH* 1960, 659) (*AR* 1960, 5).

C. W. J. Eliot investigated remains of an ancient fortification in the southern foothills of Mt. Parnes north of Acharnai and identified it as the fort of Leipsydrion occupied by the Alkmaionidai, though the existing remains are dated probably to the 4th–3rd century B.C. (*Hesperia* Suppl. XI, 58ff).

For other sites in Mt. Parnes see Phyle.

**PENTELIKON:** In 1952 I. Papadimitriou cleared a cave south of the summit. Among the finds was a 4th century B.C. relief of Pan, Dionysos, Hermes and the Nymphs (*BCH* 1953, 202) (*AR* 1952, 112).

From 1955 to 1957 Papadimitriou and Mrs. Kalogeropoulou excavated on the south slopes of the mountain (at a place called Drafi) a necropolis and ruins of the ancient deme of Phigaia. They found Geometric, Archaic and Classical graves, the remains of a large 5th century house, and other houses (*BCH* 1956, 246; 1957, 516; 1958, 681).

**PHYLE:** The fortress of Phyle, probably of the late 5th or early 4th century, lies about 3.5 km north of the village of Phyle, previously known as Chasia. It has been described by, among others, Wrede (*AM* 1924, 153ff), L. Chandler (*JHS* 46, 1926, 4ff), and F. E. Winter (*Greek Fortifications*, 1971, 139-40 and passim).

About 4 km north of the village is the Lykhnospilia cave, a cave of Pan and the Nymphs. Skias excavated in 1900–01 and found a rich deposit of Classical and later votives, some MH matt-painted pottery and Mycenaean (LH III) (*PAE* 1900, 38ff; 1901, 32ff) (*AE* 1906, 100) (cf. Ålin 111-12) (*Gazetteer* no. 384).

**PIKERMI:** Kyparissis opened three LH IIIA/B chamber tombs about one km east of the village (*AD* 11, 1927–28, *par.* 60ff) (Ålin 110) (*Gazetteer* no. 375).

**PIRAEUS:** There has been little systematic excavation in the Piraeus area; most finds have come from clearance operations before modern building construction. For the topography of the Piraeus, see:

A. Milchhöfer, *Erlaüternder Text zu den Karten von Attika*, Athens-Piraeus section, Berlin 1885.

W. Judeich, *Topographie von Athen*, 2nd ed., Munich 1931, 144ff; 425ff.

Ch. Th. Panagos, *Le Pirée*, Athens 1968, with a lengthy bibliography including a list of publications of epigraphical finds from Piraeus.

After the liberation of Athens, Piraeus, which had been virtually un-inhabited, was again built up to be the port of Athens. Ross directed excavations by the church of Ayios Nikolaos in 1834 prior to the construction of the Customs House (*Zeitscrift für Altertumswissenschaft* 1852, 113ff). Remains of ancient stoas have also been found in the area (*PAE* 1910, 134ff).

The French school with Foucart and Lechat excavated on the Eëtoneia peninsula in 1887 and located the temple of Aphrodite. There are also remains of the fortification wall built by Konon and a gate (*BCH* 1882, 540ff; 1887, 129ff; 1888, 337ff).

In Pasalimani, identified with the ancient harbour of Zea, Dragatsis carried out a number of excavations. The remains of ancient ship sheds were found around the harbour, the 2nd century B.C. theatre was excavated, the Asklepieion on the peninsula on the east side of the harbour, and on the cliffs to the east, the Serangeion, a bath complex (*Parnassos* 4, 1880, passim; 5, 1881, 1093ff; 11, 1887, 109ff: ship sheds) (*PAE* 1880–81, 47ff: theatre; 1885, 63ff; 1886, 82ff: ship sheds; 1888, 13ff: Asklepieion and Serangeion) (*AE* 1885, 62ff: theatre; 1925–26, 1ff: Serangeion). Part of the city wall and a tower, possibly of the 5th century, was found at Zea in 1967 (*AAA* 1, 1968, 113ff).

On the Kastella hill of Munychia, Dragatsis excavated various remains including the ancient theatre of Dionysos in 1880 (I. Ch. Dragatsis, *Ta Theatra tou Peiraios kai o kophos limin*, Athens, 1882). Part of the wall surrounding the hill was found in 1967, (*AAA* 1, 1968, 113ff). In 1935 I. Threpsiadis carried out excavations on the Koumoundouros headland on the western side of Tourkolimani harbour, identified with ancient

Munychia, in preparation for the construction of the Yacht Club. Part of the fortress of Hippias was found, and inscriptions identifying the site of the temple of Artemis Munychia (*PAE* 1935, 159ff).

In 1959 a group of bronze and marble statues including a late 6th century bronze kouros figure was found by workmen near the main harbour and excavated by Papadimitriou and Mastrokostas (*AR* 1958, 23; 1959, 7) (*Ergon* 1959, 161ff).

**PORTO RAPHTI (Perati and Koroni):** The Mycenaean cemetery on Perati on the north side of Porto Raphti bay is one of the most important in Attica. In 1895 Stais cleared two Mycenaean graves at a place he identified as ancient Steiria (*AE* 1895, 199ff) but it was not until 1953 that excavations to clear the necropolis were begun by S. Iakovidis. They continued through 1963. More than 200 chamber tombs were excavated. The cemetery is important for showing the continuity of LH IIIB and C in east Attica (*PAE* 1953, 88ff through *PAE* 1960) (*Ergon* 1954, 10ff through *Ergon* 1961) (*AD* 19, 1964, *Chr.* 1, 87ff) (Ålin 107ff) (Desborough 115ff) (*Gazetteer* no. 367).

The ancient fortifications on the Koroni peninsula on the south side of the bay had been described by Lolling (*AM* 1879, 351ff). In 1959 the American School under E. Vanderpool, with J. R. McCredie, A. Steinberg, and M. R. Jones of the British School mapped the site, and in 1960 carried out a short excavation with the cooperation of C. Davaras. They concluded that the fortress dates from the Chremonidean war in the 3rd century B.C. A number of coins of Ptolemy II Philadelphos were found (*Hesperia* 31, 1962, 26ff) (*AD* 16, 1960, *Chr.* 40ff) (Contrary views expressed by R. Edwards: *Hesperia* 32, 1963, 109ff, and reply in *Hesperia* 33, 1964, 69ff) (cf. *Hesperia* Suppl. XI, 1ff).

C. Vermeule reported on the investigation of the colossal statue on Raphti island, and the exploration of the smaller islands Raphtopoula and Prasonisi. Mycenaean Hellenistic and Roman sherds were noted on Raphtopoula (*Hesperia* 31, 1962, 62ff).

**RAPHINA:** Between 1951 and 1955 about 2 km south of Raphina on the Askitario hill and the slopes to the north nearer Raphina, D. Theocharis excavated a settlement and metal-working establishment dating back to the EH period. There are three EH levels, in which houses, a defense wall, and bronze smelting works were excavated. The settlement was probably destroyed by MH invaders as a small amount of MH pottery was found on the site. It was succeeded by a LH II–IIIB settlement (*PAE* 1951, 77ff; 1952, 149ff; 1953, 117ff; 1954, 113; 1955, 109ff) (*AE* 1953–54, part 3, 59ff) (Ålin 110) (*Gazetteer* no. 374).

**RHAMNOUS:** The Society of Dilettanti visited the site in 1817 and planned the Temple of Nemesis and the smaller temple known as the Temple of Themis next to it (Society of Dilettanti, *Unedited Antiquities of Attica*, 1817, 45ff). In 1880 D. Philios excavated briefly on the acropolis of the ancient town, particularly in the theatre (*PAE* 1880, 62ff). From 1890–93 M. Stais for the Archaeological Society excavated at the temples of Nemesis and Themis and published sculpture and inscriptions from the temple terrace. He also excavated on the acropolis superficially, though he had hoped to excavate it completely. He located a sanctuary of Dionysos, and a temple of the healing heroes Amphiaraos and Aristomachos on the acropolis (*PAE* 1890, 27ff; 1891, 13ff; 1892, 29ff) (*AE* 1891, 45ff).

The temples have also been examined by Orlandos in 1922–23 (*BCH* 1924, 305ff), by Zschietzschmann (*AA* 1929, 447ff), Plommer (*BSA* 45, 1950, 94ff) and by Dinsmoor (*Hesperia* 30, 1961, 179ff).

In 1947 J. Pouilloux and J. Marcadé surveyed the acropolis and the sanctuary of the healing heroes (J. Pouilloux, *La Forteresse de Rhamnonte*, Paris 1954).

Mastrokostas excavated 4th–2nd century B.C. graves east of the fortress in 1958 (*PAE* 1958, 28ff). I. Kondis and V. Petrakos worked on the site of the temple of Nemesis in 1960 (*AD* 16, 1960, *Chr.* 36ff). New fragments of the cult image were found (G. Despinis, *Symbole stin melete tou ergou tou Agorakritou*, Athens 1971, 162ff).

**SKARAMANGA:** LH III graves were excavated at Skaramanga on the Bay of Eleusis during the war (*AA* 1943, 303) (Ålin 113) (*Gazetteer* no. 385).

**SOUNION:** The temple of Poseidon at Sounion was first excavated by W. Dörpfeld in 1884. He also identified the remains of the earlier poros temple, on whose foundations the Classical temple rests (*AM* 1884, 324ff). V.

Stais, followed by A. Orlandos, excavated at intervals during the period 1897 to 1915. The Poseidon temple was long believed to be dedicated to Athena, but the Athena temple was excavated by Stais in 1898 and correctly identified by Dörpfeld. In 1906, two kouroi figures, one eleven feet tall, were found (*PAE* 1897, 16ff; 1898, 92ff; 1899, 98ff; 1908, 63) (*AE* 1900, 113ff; 1917, 213ff) (*AD* 1915, 1ff) (On the Athena temple: *PAE* 1898, 94ff) (*AE* 1900, 122ff). During the Roman period much of the superstructure of the Athena temple was removed and reused in the agora in Athens (*Agora* XIV, 166).

J. H. Young of the American School surveyed sites of probable farmsteads in the area north of Sounion (*Hesperia* 25, 1956, 122ff) (cf. *BSA* 68, 1973, 448ff).

E. J. A. Kenny has studied the docks and ship sheds on the Sounion promontory (*BSA* 42, 1947, 194ff).

See also: W. B. Dinsmoor, Jr., *Sounion*, 2nd ed., Athens 1974.

**SPATA:** In 1877 a prehistoric settlement was located on the Magoula hill near Spata. P. Stamatakis excavated two very rich Mycenaean chamber tombs on its slopes (*AM* 1877, 82ff) (*BCH* 1878, 185ff). In 1925 A. Arvanitopoulos excavated further Mycenaean graves and traces of the settlement. Remains range from EH to LH IIIC (*AA* 1926, 400) (cf. Ålin 109-10) (*Gazetteer* no. 371).

At 'Pousini' about one-half km south of the village an inscription was found of a sacred calendar and remains in the area are probably of the ancient deme of Erchia (*BCH* 1963, 603ff; E. Vanderpool, *BCH* 1965, 21ff).

In 1889–90 Stais excavated several Archaic grave tumuli in the vicinity of Spata, one near 'Vourva' about 3 km northeast of Spata on the road to Pikermi (*AD* 1889, 169f; 1890, 10ff, 105ff) (*AM* 1890, 318ff), one at 'Petreza' about an hour beyond Vourva toward Marathon (*AD* 1890, 29 and 49) and one near Velanideza on the east coast (q.v.).

**THORIKOS:** The acropolis of ancient Thorikos is on the Velatouri hill. In 1817 the Society of Dilettanti uncovered a Doric style temple of Demeter and Kore (Society of Dilettanti, *Unedited Antiquities of Athens*, 1817, 61ff). In 1886 the American School excavated the unusually shaped theatre on the slopes of the hill (*Papers of the Am. School* 4, 1885–86, 1ff).

Stais excavated on the hill in the 1890s. He excavated Mycenaean tombs and prehistoric settlement remains on the summit. MH, LH I–II, and LH IIIB material was found (*AD* 1890, 159ff) (*PAE* 1893, 12ff) (*AE* 1895, 221ff) (cf. *Gazetteer* no. 361).

In 1960 the Belgians under H. Mussche began excavations which have been continued from 1963 to the present as a joint Belgian-Greek enterprise. They first excavated the probable Peloponnesian War fortress on the Ayios Nikolaos promontory, and nearby Hellenistic mining establishments. Then excavations were concentrated on the slopes of the Velatouri hill. They found more Mycenaean tombs including two tholoi, and cemeteries containing tombs of the proto-Geometric period to the 4th century B.C. On the west, south and east slopes they excavated the industrial quarters of the Archaic and Classical city. A guide to the site and summary of the excavations has recently been published: H. F. Mussche, *Thorikos, A Guide to the Excavations*, Comité des Fouilles Belges en Grèce, Brussels 1974. Annual preliminary reports have been published regularly, though with a lag of several years, since *Thorikos, 1963*, Brussels 1968. Reports also published in *AD* (*AD* 19, 1964, *Chr.* 1, 80ff; 20, 1965 *Chr.* 1, 128ff; 21, 1966, *Chr.* 1, 108ff; 22, 1967, *Chr.* 1, 137ff; 25, 1970, *Chr.* 1, 133ff) (see also H. F. Mussche, ed., *Thorikos and the Laurion in Archaic and Classical Times, Colloquy March 1973, Miscellanea Graeca I*, State University of Ghent, 1974) (cf. *Hesperia* Suppl. XI, 33-34, for the Ayios Nikolaos promontory).

W. A. McDonald discovered a destroyed Geometric grave by chance in 1958 (*Hesperia* 30, 1961, 299ff).

**TRAKHONES:** Casual finds of LH IIIB, Geometric, Archaic and Classical vases are reported from Trakhones, about 5 km south of Athens (*BSA* 42, 1947, 4) (*Gazetteer* no. 352).

Since 1952 Geroulanos has excavated an agricultural settlement of the 5th–4th century and Hellenistic periods (*BSA* 68, 1973, 443ff, particularly on evidence for bee-keeping). He has also reported late Geometric and proto-Attic graves (*AM* 1973, 1ff).

The remains of ancient farming in this vicinity—parallel field systems and terracing—are well-illustrated with aerial photography by J. Bradford (*Ancient Landscapes, Studies in Field Archaeology*, London 1957, 29ff).

**VARI:** In 1891 Stais excavated plundered Greek tombs in the area, the site of the ancient deme of Anagyrous (*AD* 1891, 15ff).

In 1935–36, Stavropoulos excavated several walled grave enclosures of late seventh to mid-fifth century date to the north of the village. The remains were excellent and rich, but no full publication was made (*AA* 1936, 124ff; 1937, 121ff) (*BCH* 1937, 451).

In 1939 G. Oikonomos explored the ridge south of the road west of Vari and excavated a complex of small buildings, perhaps partly a shrine. He also noted Mycenaean remains. No full report was made (*AA* 1940, 177f) (Ålin 106) (*Gazetteer* no. 357) (Eliot 41f) (cf. *Hesperia* Suppl. XI, 28ff). In 1957 Papadimitriou excavated eight cist graves containing late Geometric vases (*BCH* 1958, 672).

In 1961–62 and 1964 Miss A. Andriomenou and V. Kallipolitis excavated in a mainly Archaic and Classical cemetery northwest of the town, about 800 meters south of the cemetery excavated by Stais. The tombs, with the remains of many funeral pyres, were grouped within enclosures. The earliest graves were three late Geometric cist graves (*AD* 17, 1961–62, *Chr.* 1, 37ff; 18, 1963, *Mel.* 115ff; 20, 1965, *Chr.* 1, 112ff).

The Cave of Pan and the Nymphs north of Vari was first described by R. Chandler who visited it in 1765 (*Travels in Asia Minor and Greece*, revised, 1825, 185ff). The cave was apparently decorated in the early 5th century by a certain Archidamos, who represented himself in one relief working with a hammer and chisel. The cave was excavated by the American School in 1903. It was in use from about 600 to 150 B.C. (*AJA* 7, 1903, 263ff) (cf. S. Casson, *The Technique of Early Greek Sculpture*, 1933, 95ff and passim).

In 1966 A. J. Graham, J. Ellis Jones and L. H. Sackett of the British School excavated an isolated house of the second half of the 4th century B.C. below the cave. Certain clay pots suggest that bee-keeping was practiced (*BSA* 68, 1973, 355ff). Other remains in the area are noted by C. W. J. Eliot (*Coastal Demes of Attica*, 35ff).

**VARKIZA:** At Varkiza, south of Vari, I. Papadimitriou and D. Theocharis excavated two Mycenaean chamber tombs (LH IIIA–B) and a number of child burials at the locality Kaminia (*BCH* 1954, 110). In 1960 I. Kondis and B. Petrakos excavated two more chamber tombs and six other graves (*AD* 16, 1960, *Chr.* 39) (*Antiquity* 34, 1960, 266ff) (Ålin 106) (*Gazetteer* no. 358). In 1974 P. Themelis discovered two Mycenaean chamber tombs near Kaminia, containing LH 111A2 and IIIB material (*AAA* 7, 1974, 422ff).

**VELANIDEZA:** At Velanideza east of Spata in 1889–90, Stais excavated an Archaic burial tumulus. The tumulus was surrounded by a double enclosure wall and contained nineteen tombs of probably 6th century date with black-figure vases. There were also later 5th–4th century and Roman burials made in the tumulus (*AD* 1889, 122; 1890, 5ff, 16ff).

In 1927 Kyparissis excavated five Mycenaean chamber tombs near the chapel of Ayios Soteiros. The tombs were plundered, but are of LH IIIA–B date, possibly IIIC (*AD* 1927–28, *par.* 64-65) (*AA* 1930, 10) (Ålin 110) (*Gazetteer* no. 373).

**VOULA**: On Cape Punta on the Alyki peninsula between Glyphada and Voula is a largely plundered Mycenaean chamber tomb necropolis. Keramopoulos explored some of the tombs in 1919, and also a round building of the Classical period (*PAE* 1919, 32ff) (*AA* 1920, 250ff). Between 1954 and 1957 I. Papadimitriou and D. Theocharis excavated more than twelve of the tombs and identified others. They dated from LH IIIA–C. They also discovered an EH grave (*PAE* 1954, 72ff; 1955, 78ff; 1957, 29ff) (*Ergon* 1954, 10; 1955, 24ff; 1957, 14ff).

The church of Ayios Nikolaos at Pyrnari, inland between Voula and Glyphada, is probably the center of the ancient deme of Aixone. For remains noted by Fauvel and Gropius in 1819 see Eliot (*Coast Demes of Attica*, 6ff, 17ff). A casual find of LH III vases has also been reported (*BSA* 42, 1947, 4).

For traces of ancient farming in the area, ancient field divisions and terrace walls, see J. Bradford (*Ancient Landscapes, Studies in Field Archaeology*, London 1957, 29ff).

**VOULIAGMENI:** In 1926–27 the Greek Department of Antiquities excavated the 6th century B.C. temple of Apollo Zoster on the base of the Mikro Kavouri peninsula (Cape Zoster), also finding an altar and a Roman building (*AD* 11, 1927, 9ff). In 1936 Stavropoulos excavated a building contemporary with the temple, probably either a priests' house or an inn (*AE* 1938, 1ff).

E. Varoucha-Christodoulopoulou published chance finds of Ptolemaic coins and other material found on Cape Zoster and suggested that this was the site of a Ptolemaic camp during the Chremonidean war (*AE* 1953–54, *part* 3, 321ff).

In 1958–59 E. Mastrokostas in an emergency excavation uncovered a fort on the peninsula south of the temple. He attributed most of the finds to the third millenium B.C. Only a short unofficial and not generally available report was made. However, though there was probably an EH settlement here, as Classical, Hellenistic and Roman material was also found, the date of the fortification cannot be ascertained until further material is published (*Hesperia* Suppl. XI, 30ff, with translation of short report).

At 'Palaiochori' between Voula and Vouliagmeni Archaic, Classical and Hellenistic sherds were found on a settlement site, probably the ancient deme of Halai Aixonides (Eliot, 25ff).

# Achaia

The following sites in the modern nome of Achaia would usually be considered part of ancient Arcadia: Kalavryta (Kynaitha), Kastria, Kleitor, Lousoi, Paos, and Psophis.

**AIGEIRA:** Ancient Aigeira is located at Palaiokastro southeast of the modern village of Aigeira. For bibliography of early reports see F. von Duhn (*AM* 3, 1878, 61) and Frazer (Frazer, *Pausanias* 4, 176ff). The city was partially excavated by an Austrian expedition under O. Walter in 1915–16 and again in 1925 with H. Möbius and E. Szekely. Fortification and terrace walls, and various buildings including the theatre and a temple of Zeus were discovered. A colossal head, identified with the statue of Zeus by Eukleides mentioned by Pausanias (VII 26.4) was discovered and an arm was later found by villagers (*JÖAI* 19-20, 1919, 1ff, and Beiblatt 5 ff; 27, 1932, 146ff, and Beiblatt 223ff). Although no Mycenaean material was found in these excavations, Mycenaean material had been reported as coming from Aigeira (Åström 97ff lists these finds).

The Austrian Institute with W. Alzinger and V. Leon-Mitsopoulou resumed work in 1972. Further work was done in the theatre and a Hellenistic-Roman building with a potter's kiln was excavated. Soundings were made on the southern terrace of the acropolis and evidence of occupation from LH IIIB through Hellenistic times was obtained. Work continued in 1973 (*AR* 1972–73, 18f; 1973, 18) (*AAA* 6, 1973, 193ff; 7, 1974, 157ff).

**AIGION:** The modern town of Aigion occupies the site of the ancient city and ancient remains are sparse. For early reports and bibliography see F. von Duhn (*AM* 3, 1878, 63ff) and Frazer (Frazer, *Pausanias* 4, 159ff). N. Kyparissis referred to a prehistoric cemetery at Aigion and other Mycenaean graves have been reported in the Aigion area, at 'Kallithea', west of Aigion, and possibly near Vovoda village, southwest of Aigion (Åström 99f, 109) (Papadopoulos nos. 57, 58, 60).

N. Yialouris excavated in Aigion in 1953–54, discovering a Roman building which reused 5th century material, a Classical building, a largely plundered Classical cemetery, and Roman graves. At the Psila Alonia square he found a mostly plundered Mycenaean cemetery (*PAE* 1954, 287ff) (*Ergon* 1954, 39) (*BCH* 1955, 252f).

E. Mastrokostas has reported finds of pottery ranging from Neolithic to Geometric from rescue excavations in 1965–66 within the city; also Hellenistic ware from graves and a well, and a Hellenistic pebble mosaic.

Mycenaean chamber tombs were found by the secondary school in 1967 (*AAA* 1, 1968, 136ff) (*AD* 22, 1967, *Chr.* 1, 214ff) (*AR* 1968–69, 15f). A. Papadopoulos excavated eleven more chamber tombs at this locality in 1970. Material dates from LH IIB through LH IIIC (*AD* 26, 1971, *Chr.* 1, 175ff). Chance finds are also reported, including a possibly Roman statue of a man (*AAA* 5, 1972, 496ff) (*AD* 26, 1971, *Chr.* 1, 185).

Near Vovoda village N. Yialouris reported Archaic buildings and a Geometric cemetery (*BCH* 1960, 690) (*AR* 1960, 14).

**AKHLADIES:** On the Akhouria hill near Akhladies, about 5 km south of Aigion, P. Nerantzoulis excavated a Mycenaean cemetery in the 1930s. N. Kyparissis excavated in 1939, but found the tombs plundered. It is not established whether the pottery found by Nerantzoulis is of LH IIIA, B, or C date (*PAE* 1939, 103ff). Other chance finds of Mycenaean tombs are known (Åström 96) (Papadopoulos no. 62).

**AKRATA:** A Mycenaean cemetery was reported by N. Moutsopoulos near Akrata (N. K. Moutsopoulou, "Arkhitektonika Mnimeia tis Periokhis tis Arkhaias Vouras," *Neon Athinaion* 3, 1958, 4, note 23) (cf. Papadopoulos no. 67). Near Krathi, during road work a Neolithic settlement was discovered, and an MH tomb (*AAA* 1, 1968, 136ff) (Papadopoulos no. 68).

**ARAVONITSA:** An MH tomb containing Minyan ware and hand-made pottery was opened by peasants near this village west of Aigion (*BCH* 1956, 291) (Åström 100).

**ARAXOS:** The Kastro tis Kalogrias, a Cyclopean fortification on the southernmost hill of the Mavra Vouna on the Araxos peninsula is identified as the Teichos of the Dymaeans. For early description and bibliography see Frazer (Frazer, *Pausanias* 4, 112-13). E. Mastrokostas carried out some excavations between 1962 and 1966, concentrating on the Mycenaean remains. Obsidian blades and Neolithic and EH sherds attest early occupation of the site; the fortification probably dates from LH IIIA. LH IIIB and C house remains were also excavated. The fortress was continually occupied throughout antiquity up to the Byzantine period (*PAE* for years 1962–65) (*Ergon* for years 1962–66) (*Archaeology* 15, 1962, 133ff) (*AD* 18, 1963, *Chr.* 1, 111ff; 19, 1964, *Chr.* 2, 187ff; 20, 1965, *Chr.* 2, 224ff).

**DREPANON:** Two Geometric cemeteries with pithos burials were discovered in 1970 during road building near the village; pottery, bronze vessels, pins, rings, and iron weapons and ornaments were among the finds (*AD* 26, 1971, *Chr.* 1, 185ff) (*AE* 1973, 15ff).

**DROSIA:** N. Kyparissis investigated a cemetery of Mycenaean chamber tombs in 1927–28 near this village (formerly Prostovitza) on the west slope of Mt. Erymanthos. There were over a hundred destroyed graves but few finds (*PAE* 1927, 52; 1928, 114ff) (*Gazetteer* no. 296) (Papadopoulos no. 51).

**ELIKISTRA:** Work on the road from Patras to the Gerokomeion monastery at Vakrou revealed an LH IIIA–C chamber tomb (*AD* 22, 1967, *Chr.* 1, 214).

**HELIKI:** Ancient Heliki, near the mouth of the Selinos river, was destroyed by earthquake and tidal wave in 373 B.C. Various attempts to locate the sunken city have been made, by R. Demangel in 1948 (*BCH* 1950, 272f), and by S. Dontas (*Praktika tis Akadimias Athinon* 27, 1952, 90ff). S. Marinatos summarized what is known about Heliki (*Archaeology* 13, 1960, 186ff) and searched for irregularities in the sea bed in 1966, without positive results (*AR* 1966–67, 12).

**KALAVRYTA:** Ancient Kynaitha, an Arcadian city, was perhaps located in the region of Kalavryta. The Lyssovrysis spring is perhaps the Alyssos spring mentioned by Pausanias (VIII 19, 2-3) as being two stades from the city (cf. Frazer, *Pausanias* 4, 260ff) (*RE* XI, 1922, 2480ff). Dodwell noted Doric columns north of the town (Dodwell *Tour* II, 447, 451) and Ernst Meyer reported a Hellenistic-Roman chamber tomb northwest of the city (Meyer 1939, 107ff). E. Mastrokostas has excavated in and around Kalavryta. On the slopes of the hill of the Frankish castle of Tremola which overlooks the town, he found prehistoric and Classical sherds and the remains of ancient houses, in addition to the Medieval remains. Ancient graves were found about one km east of the Kastro, at Kioupoa. Arms, including a helmet of Illyrian type, were found in a pithos burial (*AD* 22, 1967, *Chr.* 1, 130ff).

**KALLITHEA:** In 1953 N. Yialouris excavated two LH IIIC chamber tombs about one km north of Kallithea, south of Patras. In one tomb was a bronze sword, a spear head, and a unique find of a pair of bronze greaves (*BCH* 1954, 124) (*AJA* 58, 1954, 235; 64, 1960, 13f) (Åström 102) (*Archaeology* 13, 1960, 71) (*AM* 75, 1960, 42ff). Another chamber tomb has been uncovered by ploughing about 100 m southeast of the previously excavated graves (*AD* 26, 1971, *Chr.* 1, 185).

**KAMARAI:** P. Nerantzoulis found obsidian, stone tools, EH and Mycenaean sherds on the Xeriko hill on the east side of the Phoinix River ("Triantaphyllou," *Kamarais*). N. Kyparissis excavated in 1934, but finds were not reported (*PAE* 1934, 114). P. Åström noted an EH settlement in 1961, and MH and Mycenaean sherds (Åström 109). Mycenaean chamber tombs are reported at Xeriko and at 'Paliomylos' on the west side of the river (Papadopoulos nos. 53, 54).

**KANGADI:** About 15 km southwest of Kato Achaia, N. Yialouris discovered a cemetery of small Mycenaean chamber tombs outside Kangadi on the road to Riolo. Finds include a peculiar style of vase, and in one intact tomb containing two burials a necklace of gold beads, one of bone beads and spindle-whorls were found. Pottery is of LH IIIC date but some may be earlier, possibly LH IIIA or B (*BCH* 1955, 252) (*AR* 1955, 17). Other Mycenaean tombs have been found by chance near the village (*BCH* 1951, 114; 1954, 124) (Åström 102-3) (Papadopoulos no. 3).

**KASTRIA:** E. Mastrokostas has reported the find in 1965 of Neolithic and EH I sherds in a cave about one km west of this village between Kleitor and Lousoi (*AD* 22, 1967, *Chr.* 1, 216) (*AAA* 1, 1968, 136ff).

**KATARRAKTIS (formerly Lopesi, also referred to in various reports as 'deme of Pharai'):** There are a number of ancient sites, many of Bronze Age date, in the vicinity of Katarraktis, and the area must have been of major importance in the prehistoric period. West of Katarraktis, N. Kyparissis excavated a cemetery of mostly destroyed Mycenaean chamber tombs in 1920 and noted traces of a settlement on the hill above (*AE* 1919, 98f). Two more chamber tombs were later exposed by rain and N. Yialouris examined a third (*AR* 1955, 17f).

N. Zapheiropoulos began investigating the area of Katarraktis in 1952. He examined the Monasteraki and Panagitsa caves near the village. Finds were few; there were niches in the caves for dedications. Near Kyparissis' excavations he excavated two MH graves containing Minyan and matt-painted wares. Near the village he excavated two graves which contained late Geometric ware and one containing late Corinthian material (*PAE* 1952, 396ff). Another grave containing Geometric finds was excavated in 1956 (*PAE* 1956, 197ff).

On the Drakotrypa hill east of the village Zapheiropoulos discovered a prehistoric settlement in 1957. Remains of house walls were excavated, and MH, LH I–II, IIIA–C pottery was found. Some EH ware is also reported. Three child burials were found within the settlement (*PAE* 1957, 115ff; 1958, 167ff) (*Ergon* 1957, 69ff; 1958, 139ff) (*Gazetteer* no. 297) (Papadopoulos no. 33). An extensive MH settlement was noted on the Pyrgaki hill above Katarraktis but remains were scanty (*PAE* 1958, 172ff) (*Ergon* 1958, 139).

On the Ayios Athanasios hill above Rhodia village south of Katarraktis another prehistoric settlement was discovered. LH IIIB–C material was found and a large megaron-type building was excavated. A child burial was also found. The site was perhaps occupied in the MH period as well. Two Mycenaean tholos tombs, probably connected with this settlement, were excavated nearby. Both had been plundered, but one at least was datable to LH IIIB. Among the finds was a bronze dagger with an inlay of dolphins (*PAE* 1956, 193ff; 1957, 114ff; 1958, 170ff) (*Ergon* 1956, 88ff; 1957, 69ff; 1958, 139ff). Northwest of the tholos tombs at 'Ayios Georgios' Zapheiropoulos excavated traces of a settlement. Geometric and Classical wares were found, and at a lower level some hand-made ware, possibly Mycenaean. Nearby a pithos burial and a cist-grave with Geometric ware were excavated (*PAE* 1956, 195ff) (Åström 103f) (Papadopoulos nos. 33-37).

**KATO ACHAIA:** The remains of an ancient city near Kato Achaia have variously been identified as the ruins of Dyme or of Olenos. For bibliography of early reports see Frazer, (Frazer, *Pausanias* 4, 135 and 140f) N. Kyparissis excavated a rich Hellenistic tomb in a cemetery near Kato Achaia in 1921 (*AR* 1919–21, 271f). E. Mastrokostas has reported EH and LH sherds on the Boukhomata hill similar to those found at the Kastro tis Kalogrias on the Araxos peninsula (*PAE* 1963, 98).

**KERYNIA (formerly Gardena):** On the Ayios Georgios spur, northeast of this village and southwest of Rizomylo, are remains of ancient walls, building stones and sherds, including Classical sherds. The site had formerly been identified as ancient Kerynia, and the village name changed in consequence, but Kerynia is rather to be located near Mamousia (q.v.) (Frazer *Pausanias* 4, 168, with earlier bibliography) (Meyer 1939, 127) (*Gazetteer* no. 306).

**KHALANDRITSA:** Northwest of Khalandritsa at 'Ayios Vasileios', N. Kyparissis excavated three unplundered LH IIIC chamber tombs in an extensive cemetery in 1928, 1929 and 1930 (*PAE* 1928, 110ff; 1929, 86ff; 1930, 81ff). He excavated three tholos tombs at 'Troubes' above Ayios Vasileios. In addition to Mycenaean pottery, bronze items and Geometric vases were found in the middle tomb (*PAE* 1929, 89ff; 1930, 83ff; 1956, 198ff). A Mycenaean settlement to which these tombs probably belong was located at 'Ayios Antonios' north of the village by R. Hope

Simpson (*Gazetteer* no. 293). On the Agrapidies hills east of the town Kyparissis excavated some cist tombs of perhaps LH I–II date. To the right of the road from Patras about 2 km before Khalandritsa, on a hill also called Troube he noted a large peribolos of a destroyed and plundered tomb (*PAE* 1930, 85). About one km northwest of this at 'Skoros' E. Mastrokostas has reported cist graves of the late Geometric period within burial mounds. He also noted a pithos burial near 'Ayios Vasileios' (*AD* 17, 1961–62, *Chr.* 129) (*AR* 1961, 12) (cf. Åström 100f) (Papadopoulos no. 22-25).

**KLEITOR:** The ruins of ancient Kleitor lie at 'Zagoritsa' or 'Palaiopolis' at the junction of the Karnesi and Kleitor rivers, between modern Kleitor and Kato Kleitoria (formerly Mazeika). For description and bibliography of early travellers, see Frazer (Frazer, *Pausanias* 4, 266ff). It has been more recently described by G. Papandreou (*PAE* 1920, 96ff). The Italians explored a cemetery at Kleitor in 1940 (*AR* 1939–45, 83).

**KRINI:** Some Mycenaean chamber tombs have been reported from the village of Krini, about 6 km south of Patras. One, opened in 1958, produced LH IIIB–C vases (*AD* 17, 1961–62, *Chr.* 129).

**LEONTION:** Ancient Leontion had been identified with a site to the south of Gourzoumisa (or Gourzoumistra), since renamed Leontion. The site occupies the hills of Ayios Andreas and of Ayios Konstantinos slightly higher to the east. The settlement was examined by N. Kyparissis in 1931. The site may go back to the Mycenaean period, though the visible remains are later (*PAE* 1931, 72f) (cf. Frazer, *Pausanias* 4, 155f). Ernst Meyer re-examined the site and concluded that it was too small to have been Leontion (Meyer 1939, 116ff and plan VII). Ancient Leontion is probably the site at Kastritsi north of Ayios Vlasios, previously identified as Tritaia (see Vlasia).

Kyparissis excavated a number of Mycenaean graves in the area of Gourzoumisa between 1930 and 1932, at 'Koutreika', 'Ayios Ioannis', and 'Vrayianika'. Most of the graves had been destroyed. Identifiable remains were of LH IIIB–C date (*PAE* 1930, 88; 1931, 71ff; 1932, 57ff).

**LOUSOI:** The site of ancient Lousoi is near modern Lousoi (formerly Soudena). For early bibliography and discussion of the location, see Frazer (Frazer, *Pausanias* 4, 258ff). Between 1897 and 1899 W. Dörpfeld and an Austrian expedition explored the site and in 1901 the Austrians excavated several buildings including a temple of Artemis (*JÖAI* 4, 1901, 1ff).

**MAGEIRA:** E. Mastrokostas has reported a Mycenaean tomb at 'Paliometocho' near Mageira, about 8 km south of Kamarai (*AD* 16, 1960, *Chr.* 145ff).

**MAMOUSIA:** N. Kyparissis mentioned the possibility of a Mycenaean cemetery near Mamousia but there are no reports of any actual discovery or excavation (*PAE* 1938, 119; 1939, 104) (cf. Åström 105). On a hill near Derveni, north of Mamousia, are the ruins of a city formerly identified as ancient Bura. For early bibliography and descriptions see F. von Duhn (*AM* 3, 1878, 62) and Frazer (Frazer, *Pausanias* 4, 168f). The site was visited and described by Ernst Meyer who concluded that it was probably ancient Kerynia (Meyer 1939, 127ff; Meyer 1957, 80ff). J. K. Anderson visited the site in 1950 and excavated in 1951, in conjunction with the Greek Archaeological Service. He supports Meyer's identification of the site as Kerynia (*BSA* 48, 1953, 154ff). Other finds from the site, including fragments of late Roman sculpture have been reported (*AD* 19, 1964, *Chr.* 2, 187). N. Zapheiropoulos reported the discovery of a burial pithos containing 12 Geometric vases (*PAE* 1952, 406) (*AR* 1951, 99), and Hellenistic graves have been reported from near 'Ayios Konstantinos' (*AD* 26, 1971, *Chr.* 1, 186).

**MANESI:** In 1930 N. Kyparissis excavated some Mycenaean chamber tombs in a cemetery discovered the previous year. The tombs had been plundered and largely destroyed, but some LH IIIC vases were found (*PAE* 1929, 91; 1930, 87ff) (Åström 106). There are perhaps a few tombs in the village itself (cf. Papadopoulos nos. 44-45).

**MARITSA:** Remains of an ancient temple were noted by the fork of the road to the Monastery of Maritsa from Santomeri (*AD* 22, 1967, *Chr.* 1, 216).

**MIKROS BODIAS:** At 'Bartholomio' in 1931, P. Nerantzoulis excavated one of several tholos tombs. He found three pithoi containing skeletons, beads and bronze and iron fragments. They are possibly late Mycenaean, but more likely post-Mycenaean (*AA* 1932, 142ff) (cf. Åström 106). At Loboka, on the river Selinos, N. Kyparissis excavated three Mycenaean chamber tombs in 1933. One was unplundered and produced LH IIIC vases (*PAE* 1933, 90ff; 1934, 114) (*BCH* 1935, 259) (Åström 105). Finds have also been reported from a Roman site near Mouriki (*AD* 22, 1967, *Chr.* 1, 215).

**MIRALI:** South of Mirali, off the road between Khalandritsa and Katarraktis, N. Zapheiropoulos discovered two MH tombs in 1952 (*BCH* 1953, 215) (*PAE* 1952, 398ff).

**MITOPOLIS:** N. Kyparissis noted an LH settlement and largely destroyed cemetery at Mitopolis (*PAE* 1929, 91). E. Mastrokostas reported another Mycenaean cemetery at 'Prophitis Elias' from which some bronzes were recovered (*AD* 17, 1961–62, *Chr.* 129f) (Åström 106) (Papadopoulos nos. 27-28).

**OLENOS:** Ancient Olenos is sometimes identified with a site near Kato Achaia (q.v.) also identified as ancient Dyme. E. Meyer has suggested that the site of Olenos may lie to the west of Tsoukalaïka village on the coast east of Kato Achaia where ancient remains, including Roman mosaics, have been found (Meyer 1939, 119ff) (Bölte, "Olenos," *RE* 17, 1937, 2435f).

**PAOS (formerly Skoupio):** The site of ancient Paos, already ruined by Pausanias' day (VIII 23.9), is located on the Skoupitsi hill near the village. The remains, including fortification walls, have been described by G. Papandreou (*PAE* 1920, 121ff).

**Davidson College Library**

**PATRAS:** Modern Patras occupies the site of the ancient city and remains are consequently sparse. For early bibliography and finds, see F. von Duhn (*AM* 3, 1878, 66ff), A. Milchhöfer (*AM* 4, 1879, 125ff) and Frazer (Frazer, *Pausanias* 4, 143ff). A castle occupies the ancient acropolis, perhaps also a Mycenaean site. Below the castle is the well-preserved Roman Odeon, the largest in Greece outside Athens. It was excavated in 1889 (*AD* 1889, 62ff) (*AJA* 5, 1889, 378). E. Stikas supervised the reconstruction of the skene in 1938 (*AR* 1938–39, 198) and N. Zapheiropoulos cleared the stage area in 1957 (*PAE* 1957, 112ff). Further excavation and reconstruction was carried out in 1960 (*AD* 16, 1960, *Chr.* 136ff). N. Zapheiropoulos conducted soundings in the castle and found part of an apsidal Roman building (*AR* 1949–50, 242). In 1955, N. Yialouris examined a tower of the ancient city wall (*AR* 1955, 17). Rescue excavations in Patras have been reported by E. Mastrokostas and Ph. Petsas (*AD* 17, 1961–62, *Chr.* 126ff; 19, 1964, *Chr.* 2, 184ff; 20, 1965, *Chr.* 2, 221ff; 22, 1967, *Chr.* 1, 213ff; 25, 1970, *Chr.* 1, 198ff; 26, 1971, *Chr.* 1, 149ff).

A number of Hellenistic and Roman graves have been reported on the east side of the city and by the Second Girl's Secondary School (*AD* 19, loc. cit.; 25, loc. cit.). A luxurious Roman building was excavated in Psila Alonia square. Mosaics and fragmentary sculptures were recovered (*AD* 26, loc. cit.).

A Mycenaean chamber tomb with LH IIIB–C pottery was excavated by the Gerokomeio monastery in 1965; also Classical and later tombs (*AD* 22, loc. cit.). Several Mycenaean cemeteries have been reported in the Patras area. On the Koukoura hill a few km southeast of Patras behind the Achaia-Klauss wine factory N. Kyparissis excavated 12 fine and rich Mycenaean chamber tombs of LH IIIB–C2 date. The site is variously called 'Antheia', 'Klauss', 'Skondras' or 'Lopesi-Englukas' in reports (*PAE* 1936, 95ff; 1937, 84ff; 1938, 118ff; 1939, 104ff) (Ålin 63ff) (*Gazetteer* no. 289) (Papadopoulos no. 12). Kyparissis also located Mycenaean cemeteries of the same date on the hills east of Patras at 'Aroe Mesatis' and 'Samakia' (*PAE* 1933, 92ff; 1934, 114ff; 1936, 95ff). On the city generally see: S. N. Thomopoulou, *Istoria tis Poleos Patron apo Arkhaiotaton Khronon Mekhri 1821*, Patrai 1950, and K. N. Triantaphyllou, *Istorikon Lexikon ton Patron*, Patrai 1959.

**PHARAI (formerly Lalikosta):** Ancient Pharai is most likely to be identified with a site near the modern village of Pharai, about 500 m from the left bank of the Peiros River, formerly the Kamenitsa. For bibliography and discussion see Frazer (Frazer, *Pausanias* 4, 152), and Bölte (Bölte,

"Phara," *RE* 19, 1938, 1796ff). N. Zapheiropoulos opened one of many grave mounds, of uncertain date, in the plain of Pharai, south of the Peiros River. The location was not specified more closely. Two cist graves and two pithos burials were found in it (*PAE* 1957, 117) (*BCH* 1958, 726) (Åström 104).

**PHLABOURA:** At 'Velviniko' near this village west of Kalavryta, late Geometric vessels were recovered from a pithos burial in 1965 (*AD* 22, 1967, *Chr.* 1, 215f).

**PHOSTAINA:** About 7 km southeast of Kato Achaia, Mycenaean tombs were noted in the region between Phostaina, Elaiokhorio and Lousika (*AR* 1961, 12) (Papadopoulos no. 5).

**PLATANOVRYSIS (formerly Mentzena):** In 1932 N. Kyparissis examined a previously discovered cemetery near this village northwest of Khalandritsa. The tombs were plundered and destroyed. Four LH vases were recovered (*PAE* 1930, 88; 1932, 61). E. Mastrokostas has reported another Mycenaean cemetery at 'Kamini' (*AD* 17, 1961–62, *Chr.* 129) (Åström 106) (Papadopoulos nos. 20-21). He also excavated an early Geometric grave at the same location (*AD* 19, 1964, *Chr.* 2, 186).

**PORTES:** E. Mastrokosatas has reported on Neolithic sherds recovered in a cave near this village on the southwest slopes of Mt. Skollis in 1965 (*AD* 22, 1967, *Chr.* 1, 216) (*AAA* 1, 1968, 138).

**POURNARI:** An LH tholos has been reported near Pournari, about 13 km southeast of Kato Achaia (Papadopoulos no. 4).

**PRIOLITHOS:** At 'Lakkoma' near Priolithos, south of Kalavryta, a proto-

Geometric tomb found in 1966 has been reported by E. Mastrokostas (*AD* 22, 1967, *Chr.* 1, 217).

**PSOPHIS:** The remains of ancient Psophis are located near Tripotamia southwest of modern Psophis. For description and early bibliography see Frazer (Frazer, *Pausanias* 4, 282-83). It has more recently been described by G. Papandreou (*PAE* 1920, 130ff). Remains include fortification walls and temple foundations.

Kh. Kardara and G. Papadaki excavated the sanctuary of Aphrodite Erykine for the Greek Archaeological Society in 1968 and 1969, on Mt. Aphrodision. They uncovered the foundation of the main temple and two smaller ones, the telesterion, metal-workers workshops, a fountain, and the sacred road leading from Psophis. They also located the stadium (*PAE* 1968, 12ff; 1969, 73ff) (*Ergon* 1968, 12ff; 1969, 36ff).

**RYPES:** In 1871 Lebegue discovered and described an ancient site on the Trapeza hill about 7 km southwest of Aigion, near the villages of Khadzi and Koumari (*Bulletin de l' école française d' Athènes* 1, 1871, 233ff) (cf. von Duhn, *AM* 3, 1878, 66). There are remains of fortification walls, terrace walls and buildings. It is normally identified with ancient Rypes, though other locations for this city have been proposed. For discussion see Frazer (Frazer, *Pausanias* 4, 159), Bölte ("Rypes," *RE* IA, 1914, 1288ff) and E. Meyer (Meyer 1939, 123ff and plan VIII). P. Nerantzoulis excavated in 1933 with A. Papatheodorou, but the finds were never published. He excavated some Mycenaean chamber tombs and found what he termed a 'Cyclopean' wall. He felt that this site was too close to Aigion to have been Rypes and suggested that it was the acropolis of Aigion itself. The site has since been investigated by N. Kyparissis, who located the chamber tombs but found them plundered (*PAE* 1938, 119; 1939, 103) and by Åström who in 1961 concluded that the 'Cyclopean' wall was a post-Mycenaean construction. He found sherds of Geometric and later periods on the site (Åström 108).

**SIKHAINA (and surroundings):** In 1923–24 N. Kyparissis excavated eight Mycenaean chamber tombs in a largely destroyed cemetery at 'Agrapidia' east of Ano Sikhaina near Bala village. Finds were poor and have not been published; vases were of LH IIIC1–2 date (*AA* 1925, 334ff) (*BCH* 1923, 512; 1924, 472) (cf. *PAE* 1933, 92).

In 1960 N. Yialouris excavated two Mycenaean chamber tombs east of Ano Sikhaina, near Voudeni village, apparently not in the cemetery excavated by Kyparissis, and he noted a ruined chamber tomb cemetery west of Ano Sikhaina (*AD* 16, 1960, *Chr.* 137f) (*BCH* 1961, 682) (Åström 97) (Papadopoulos nos. 10-11 with sketch of locations).

From a tomb on the Anemos hill in Ano Sikhaina came 6th century vases and an Archaic terracotta figurine of a woman (*AR* 1955, 17).

**SKOURA:** E. Mastrokostas has reported a Mycenaean cist tomb found by chance near Skoura, near the border of Elis. LH IIIA and possibly B pottery was recovered (*AD* 16, 1960, *Chr.* 144f) (Åström 107f).

**STAROKHORI (formerly Lalousi, also referred to as Kalousi):** N. Kyparissis reported a Mycenaean chamber tomb near this village southwest of Khalandritsa, but apparently it was not excavated (*PAE* 1933, 91f) (Åström 105) (Papadopoulos no. 29).

**THEA (formerly Tsaplanaiïka):** In 1934 and 1935 N. Kyparissis excavated LH IIIB–C chamber tombs on the Ayios Nikolaos hill about 200 m south of Thea village, south of Patras, and at Pavlokastro, southwest of Thea (*PAE* 1934, 115; 1935, 70ff) (Åström 109).

**TRITAIA:** The site of ancient Tritaia is probably at 'Panagia' by Ayia Marina, though it was previously located at 'Kastritsi' north of Ayios Vlasios, now identified as Leontion. For discussion, see E. Meyer ("Tritaia," *RE* VII A, 1939, 237ff) and K. Triantaphyllou (Triantaphyllou "Tritaia").

**TSOUKALAIïKA:** Mycenaean tombs have been reported near this village on the coast about 14 km southwest of Patras, but apparently no excavation took place (*BCH* 1954, 124) (Aström 109) (Papadopoulos no. 7). The site of Olenos (q.v.) may lie to the west of the village.

**VLASIA:** Ancient Leontion is most probably located at 'Kastritsi' north of Ayios Vlasios near Kato Vlasia. The site had formerly been identified as Tritaia. For older bibliography see Frazer (Frazer, *Pausanias* 4, 155-56) and F. von Duhn (*AM* 3, 1878, 70). E. Meyer described the remains and discussed the identification, concluding that it was probably Leontion (Meyer 1939, 111ff and plan VI). N. Yialouris excavated the site in 1954 and 1957–58. Archaic material was found, but the city, including the theatre and walls, appears to have been rebuilt in the 4th century and destroyed by fire toward the end of the 3rd century B.C. Mycenaean sherds were reported from the slopes (*BCH* 1955, 252; 1958, 725; 1959, 620) (*AR* 1955, 17; 1959, 11). An Archaic bronze greave was found in a tomb near Menykhtaïka village (*BCH* 1959, 620) (*AR* 1959, 11). For other sites to the north of this area, see Mikros Bodias.

**VRAKHNAIÏKA:** A Mycenaean tomb was reported near this village on the coast southwest of Patras in 1954 (*BCH* 1954, 124). In 1955 N. Yialouris, N. Zapheiropoulos and A. Liagouras excavated a Mycenaean chamber tomb at 'Ayios Pendeleimon' (*BCH* 1956, 291) (*AR* 1955, 17) (Åström 109).

**VRISARION (formerly Kato Goumenitsa):** In 1925–27 N. Kyparissis excavated a number of Mycenaean chamber tombs on the Ayia Paraskevi hill west of Vrisarion. LH IIIA–B vases were found (*PAE* 1925, 43ff; 1926, 130ff) (*AD* 9, 1924–25, *par.* 14ff) (Åström 104). N. Yialouris excavated an LH I tomb in the vicinity in 1959, and two further LH III chamber tombs in 1960 (*AR* 1959, 12; 1961, 12) (*AD* 16, 1960, *Chr.* 138).

# Arcadia

**AGIORGITIKA (Mantineias):** In 1928 C. Blegen excavated a low Neolithic mound to the east of the village. Remains of dwellings, stone implements and some fragments of figurines were recovered. EH bothroi (pits) were also found in the mound (*AJA* 32, 1928, 533f).

Various ancient remains have been noted in the mountains east and north of Agiorgitika; some of them no doubt are remains of the shrines mentioned by Pausanias (VIII 54.5) in the border area between Tegea and the Argolid, though certain identification is difficult. In 1890 V. Bérard of the French School excavated foundations of two sanctuaries, possibly of Demeter and Dionysos, and recovered a fragmentary Archaic statue of a seated female (*BCH* 1890, 382ff). Another sanctuary, perhaps of Artemis, was also excavated by the French School (*AD* 1888, 121; 1889, 154f). For various other remains in the vicinity see Frazer (Frazer, *Pausanias* 4, 445ff).

**ALEA (Mantineias):** A Mycenaean site has been noted in the region of Alea, about 5 km southeast of the village, by the Ayia Sotira church on the Sarandapotamos river. The site is known as Palaiokhori or Synoikismos. LH II–IIIB and possibly EH sherds were noted in 1957 (*BSA* 56, 1961, 130 note 119). About 500 m to the southwest K. Romaios had excavated one of several tholos-shaped tombs, finding LH IIIA pottery. The excavation was not fully published (*BCH* 1921, 403) (K. A. Romaios, *Mikra Meletimata*, Thessaloniki 1958, 171) (Ålin 74) (*Gazetteer* no. 90) (Howell no. 32).

For the temple of Alea Athena, see Tegea.

**AMYGDALEA (Gortynias):** In 1937 Ernst Meyer identified a site at the Ayia Paraskevi chapel by Glanitza, since renamed Amygdalea, as an ancient sanctuary (Meyer, 1939, 52ff). In 1939 the French School with H. Metzger excavated the site. It was an isolated simple sanctuary, consisting of a temenos and altar which date back to the Archaic period, late 7th or early 6th century. After a period of disuse the terrace was enlarged and the existing altar built, probably in the 4th century. Some poor offerings were recovered (*BCH* 1940–41, 5ff).

**ASEA (Mantineias):** In 1936–38 a Swedish expedition under E. J. Holmberg excavated the site of ancient Asea at 'Palaiokastro' near Kato Asea (formerly Frankovrysi), about 5 km southeast of modern Asea (formerly Kandreva). A prehistoric settlement was uncovered, ranging from early Neolithic through EH and MH. The EH settlement had been burnt. There is some evidence for a LH I–II and LH IIIB settlement, and a few Geometric sherds. There were also a few LH and proto-Geometric or Geometric graves on the hill. The site seems to have then been uninhabited until the Hellenistic city was built. Houses and a temple were excavated (E. J. Holmberg, *The Swedish Excavations at Asea in Arcadia*, Göteborg 1944) (*Gazetteer* no. 91) (Howell no. 51). K. Romaios investigated a number of sanctuary sites in the area of Asea and excavated the Sanctuary of Saviour Athena and Poseidon mentioned by Pausanias (VIII 44.4), at 'Vigla' east of Asea in 1910, 1917, and 1958. The temple was probably built in the late 6th century, though there was probably a late 7th century predecessor (*AD* 4, 1918, 102ff) (*PAE* 1910, 274ff) (*AE* 1957, 114ff).

**AYIOS ANDREAS (Kynourias):** In 1962 Th. Karageorga in a trial excavation found a Roman fortification wall on the Nisi hill on the coast.

Further north, toward the Bay of Astros, on the Khersonisi hill where obsidian and MH and LH sherds had previously been noted (*BSA* 55, 1961, 131) she found EH pottery, MH sherds and a few Geometric sherds (*AD* 18, 1963, *Chr.* 1, 89f).

**AYIOS IOANNIS (Gortynias):** In 1930 A. Philadelpheus excavated at the site of ancient Heraia, east of the junction of the Alpheios and Ladon Rivers, by the village of Ayios Ioannis. He uncovered the peribolos wall and part of the foundations of a temple. He also excavated several rooms, two with mosaics, and remains of baths, all probably belonging to a Roman villa. He located part of an aqueduct and the necropolis (*AD* 14, 1931–32, 57ff).

**BERTSIA (Gortynias):** From Bertsia on the Ladon a torso of a Hellenistic statue, most likely of Asclepios, and probably the same as the statue previously reported (*AD* 1, 1915, 89), was reported again, along with other material indicating a sanctuary in the vicinity (Meyer 1939, 98ff) (*BCH* 1954, 130) (*AR* 1956, 15) (Meyer 1957, 18ff).

**DIMITRA (Gortynias):** In 1891 V. Leonardos excavated several sites near the Ladon River in hopes of locating places mentioned by Pausanias (VIII 25). For a description of the area, see Frazer (Frazer, *Pausanias* 4, 289ff). About 2 km southeast of Dimitra (formerly Divritsi), he uncovered the foundations of a long narrow temple, 16.80 m by 5.80 m. Among the finds was a bowl inscribed "to the maiden" (*KORAI*), and the temple may be either a temple of Demeter or of Athena (*AD* 1891, 98) (*PAE* 1891, 23ff) (cf. *AE* 1965, *Chr.* 6ff for a comparison of various temples in northern Gortynia). See Vakhlia and Voutsi.

In 1939 roadworks revealed prehistoric remains on the Troupes or Damara hill about 2 km northeast of the village. K. Syriopoulos has several times investigated the site. It was inhabited intensively and continuously from the Neolithic period until LH IIIC2. He would identify it as Homeric Enispe (*BSA* 68, 1973, 193ff).

**GORTYS:** The site of ancient Gortys at Astikholo has been excavated by the French School, in 1941–42 under R. Martin and H. Metzger, in 1950–52 by H. Metzger, P. Courbin, and R. Ginouvès, and in 1954–55 by Ginouvès and T. Reekmans. The acropolis fortifications were partially excavated and studied in 1941–42. The large circuit is probably a refortification of the acropolis at the time of the foundation of Megalopolis (c. 370 B.C.). On the south side is a smaller circuit, probably of the 2nd century B.C. In 1941 a sanctuary of Asclepios with a late 5th–early 4th century temple was explored below the acropolis. In 1942 another temple, also of Asclepios was located by the Ayios Andreas chapel above the ravine of the Lousios River north of the city (*BCH* 1940–41, 274ff; 1942–43, 334ff;

1947–48, 81ff). Excavation in the 1950s concentrated on the second, larger, sanctuary. The temple is probably of the 4th century B.C. A bath complex probably Hellenistic, including a round room with nine bath cubicles, was excavated. Other buildings uncovered included houses, a potter's kiln with Roman pottery, and an originally 5th century building with a tiled channel leading to a room with a mosaic floor. The fortifications of the sanctuary complex were also studied (*BCH* 1951, 130ff; 1952, 245ff; 1953, 263ff; 1955, 335ff; 1956, 399ff) (R. Ginouvès, *L'Établissement thermal de Gortys d'Arcadie,* École française d'Athènes, *Études Péloponnésiennes* II, Paris 1959).

**HELLINIKO (Gortynias):** P. Charneux and R. Ginouvès have reported on a survey of fortifications in the area of ancient Gortys carried out in 1955 and 1956. At Helliniko (formerly Moulatsi) they examined a small fortress, probably Archaic (*BCH* 1956, 523 and 542ff).

**KALLIANI (Gortynias):** In 1937 E. Meyer noted the remains of a sanctuary west of Kalliani, about one km east of the Ladon (Meyer 1939, 45ff). In 1954 he explored the area between Kalliani and the river with F. Eckstein and made a test excavation about 2 km west of the village; a fuller excavation was made in 1955, uncovering the remains of a Roman villa. Between this excavation and the town a necropolis was located, and various remains of late Classical–early Hellenistic date including parts of terracotta acroteria, probably indicating that there was a temple nearby, around the Ayios Georgios chapel (Meyer 1957, 11ff) (*AM* 75, 1960, 9ff). Tombs of probably Mycenaean date have been reported from the vicinity (*AR* 1959, 10).

**KAMENITSA (Gortynias):** In 1966 a cave was uncovered by workmen 800 m south of Kamenitsa. Bones and Neolithic sherds were collected by K. Dimakopoulou (*AD* 22, 1967, *Chr.* 1, 203). North of Kamenitsa, about one km east of Karvouni village on the Sphakovouni hill, E. Meyer noted a site he identified as ancient Torthyneion ( Meyer 1939, 37ff). R. Howell in 1963 noted MH and Mycenaean sherds, and a Medieval tower, but nothing in between (Howell no. 45).

**KHOTOUSSA (Mantineias):** The remains of Hellenistic and Roman

Kaphyai are at 'Ayiannis' south of the village. It has been described by F. Hiller von Gärtringen and H. Latterman (*Arkadische Forschungen*, Berlin 1911, 21ff) and G. Papandreou (*PAE* 1920, 114ff). About 500 m southeast of this, on the Ayios Georgios hill, R. Howell in 1963 found prehistoric sherds of indefinite period and obsidian fragments. Classical and Hellenistic sherds were also found, and this hill was perhaps the predecessor of the Hellenistic city to the northwest (Howell no. 1).

**KOSMAS (Kynourias):** A chance find of weapons, probably from a sanctuary or votive deposit, has been reported from near Kosmas (*BCH* 1960, 693). On Mount Profitis Elias west of Kosmas Kh. Khristou in a trial excavation found evidence of a probably Archaic fort guarding the pass (*BCH* 1963, 759) (*AD* 18, 1963, *Chr.* 1, 87f) (cf. *BSA* 15, 1908–9, 165).

**KYNOURIA (Eparchy of):** Kynouria as a whole has seen little archaeological work. Sites have been noted by W. Wrede (*AA* 1927, 364), A. J. B. Wace and F. W. Hasluck (*BSA* 15, 1908–9, 158ff), and R. Hope Simpson and H. Waterhouse (*BSA* 56, 1961, 130ff). Among the more important is Plaka, the port of Leonidi, where fortifications, terrace walls, and tombs of a Classical city, probably Prasiai (Brasiai) have been noted. Obsidian, prehistoric sherds including LH III as well as Classical remains have been noted at Mari, the site of ancient Maries.

In addition to his excavations at Analipsis near Vouvoura, K. Romaios has noted other sites including a possible sanctuary site at Mone Loukous northwest of Astros, and stone cairns, probably marking the Laconian border, between Ayios Petros and Arakhova (*PAE* 1911, 254; 1950, 235ff) (*BSA* 11, 1904–5, 137f).

Excavations of the following sites are listed separately: Ayios Andreas, Kosmas, Palaiokhori, and Vouvoura (Analipsis).

**KYPARISSIA (Gortynias):** In 1893 A. G. Bather and V. W. Yorke conducted brief excavations in the vicinity of Kyparissia, northwest of Megalopolis, in order to locate the sites of Bathos and Basilis mentioned by Pausanias (VIII 29). At 'Vathy Revma' below the chapel of Ayios Georgios, a group of votives, terracotta figurines and some bronzes, small pots and lamps, the latest probably of the 4th century B.C., indicated a shrine, probably of the Great Goddess Pausanias mentioned. East of Kyparissia what was apparently a road lined with statue bases was excavated. It probably led up to the acropolis of Basilis (*JHS* 13, 1892–93, 227ff). K. Stephanos excavated at the shrine in 1907, finding small votive pigs and a bronze statuette, probably of the Great Goddess (*PAE* 1907, 123f).

**MT. LYKAION:** Some of the sanctuaries mentioned by Pausanias (VIII 38.2ff) on Mt. Lykaion near Lykosoura have been investigated. The altar and precinct of Lykaion Zeus were excavated by K. Kontopoulos in 1897 and K. Kourouniotis in 1902. Bones, bronze tripods, iron knives and bronze statuettes were among the finds (*PAE* 1903, 50) (*AE* 1904, 152ff). The sanctuary of Parrasian Apollo is probably that sanctuary excavated by Kourouniotis at 'Sta Marmara' above Isoma Karyon in 1903 (*PAE* 1903, 51) (*AE* 1910, 29ff). The stadium of the sanctuary of Pan was also investigated in 1903 at 'Kato Kampo' (*PAE* 1903, 51).

**LYKOSOURA (Megalopoleos):** The Sanctuary of Despoina, the 'Mistress', on a hill east of the village of Lykosoura (formerly Stala), was excavated by V. Leonardos and P. Kavvadias in 1889–90 and 1895. They uncovered the temple and recovered large fragments of the cult statues by Damophon, usually dated to the 2nd century B.C., though the temple may originally date from the 4th century. Votive terracottas including animal-headed dancers were found, and altars, a stoa, and a hall of initiation were also excavated (*AD* 1889 passim; 1890, passim) (*PAE* 1896, 93ff) (*AE* 1895, 263ff; 1896, 101ff) (P. Kavvadias, *Fouilles de Lycosoura* I, Athens 1893) (Frazer, *Pausanias* 4, 367ff, has good descriptions and bibliography) (On the statues: G. Dickens, *BSA* 12, 1905–6, 109ff; 13, 1906–7, 356ff; 17, 1910–11, 80ff) (K. Kourouniotis, *Katalogos tou Mouseiou Lykosouras*, Athens 1911).

E. Lévy of the French School carried out some soundings around the cella in 1966 and recommended redating Damophon to the period of Hadrian (*BCH* 1967, 518ff). Between 1969 and 1972 Lévy and J. Marcadé restudied all the fragments of the sculptures. They discuss the restoration, but come to no final conclusion on the date (*BCH* 1972, 967ff). Lykosoura city, little explored, is to the west of the sanctuary.

**MANTINEIA:** The site of Mantineia is about 14 km north of Tripolis.

The city had been synoicized from local villages probably about 500 B.C., was destroyed in 385 B.C. by the Spartans, and restored about 371 B.C. Most of the material from the city dates after this. The site was excavated by the French School under G. Fougères with V. Bérard in 1887–89. The fortifications were examined, and the agora, theatre and temple of Hera were uncovered. One of the chief discoveries was a series of pedestal re- liefs of Apollo, Marsyas and the Muses mentioned by Pausanias (VIII 9.1) (*BCH* 1887, 485ff; 1888, 105ff; 1890, 65ff) (G. Fougères, *Mantinée et l'Arcadie orientale*, Paris 1898). Fougères also explored the area around Mantineia attempting to locate monuments mentioned by ancient authors (*BCH* 1890, 76ff).

Th. Karageorga conducted trial excavations on the Gourtsouli hill, probably Ptolis, the acropolis of the predecessor of Classical Mantineia. Geometric sherds were found, and a small sanctuary was excavated with votive terracottas, mainly Archaic, and other finds ranging from Geometric to Hellenistic (*AD* 18, 1963, *Chr.* 1, 88f). Mycenaean sherds, a possibly Cyclopean wall, and Archaic cist graves had previously been noted by R. Hope Simpson (*Gazetteer* no. 87).

**MAVRIKION (Mantineias):** The shrine of Artemis Knakeatis outside the city of Tegea towards Laconia (Pausanias VIII 53.11) was excavated in 1907 by K. Romaios at 'Psili Korphi' near Mavrikion. It is a small Doric temple dating from about 700 (*PAE* 1907, 120ff) (*AE* 1952, 1ff).

**MEGALOPOLIS:** Ancient Megalopolis, founded in 370 B.C., lies to the north of the modern town, and is bisected by the Helisson River. It was excavated between 1890 and 1893 by the British School under W. Loring, G. C. Richards, W. J. Woodhouse, E. F. Benson and E. A. Gardner. On the north side of the river the main excavation was of the agora, the stoa of Philip, the temenos of Zeus Soter and the archives. On the south side, the theatre, and a public building, probably the Thersilium or senate house were excavated (*JHS* 11, 1890, 294ff; 13, 1892–93, 319ff; 356ff) (E. A. Gardner et al., *Excavations at Megalopolis 1890–91, JHS* Supplement no. 1, 1892) (cf. Frazer, *Pausanias* 4, 317ff for description and plans). In 1901 Roman buildings were excavated by M. Kavallieratos of the Greek Archaeological Society (*PAE* 1901, 45ff). Clearance and supplementary excavations of the theater were carried out by E. Stikas and Kh. Khristou in 1962–63 (*PAE* 1962, 178f; 1963, 218). Also see the monograph by A. Petronatis (*Megale Polis in Arkadia, Ancient Greek Cities* no. 23, Athens Cen- ter of Ekistics, Athens 1973, in modern Greek).

**METHYDRION (Gortynias):** At the site of ancient Methydrion circuit walls and the possible remains of a temple by a chapel within the walls have been noted, and the remains of another temple in the valley outside the walls (Frazer, *Pausanias* 4, 362-63). The Greek Archaeological Society explored the site and planned to excavate the temple, perhaps the temple of Horse Poseidon mentioned by Pausanias (VIII 36. 1-2) but apparently no excavation took place (*PAE* 1858–59, 211).

**NEA EKKLISSOULA (Megalopoleos):** In 1961 Th. Karageorga in a trial excavation at Nea Ekklissoula (formerly Mertze) north of Megalopolis, uncovered the foundations of an Archaic temple. A number of 7th–6th century votives including weapons, were found (*AD* 17, 1961–62, *Chr.* 86ff).

**NOMIAN MOUNTAINS:** K. Kourouniotis identified a sanctuary he found south of Lykosoura as the sanctuary of Nomian Pan mentioned by Pausanias (VIII 38.11) (*PAE* 1902, 72ff).

**ORCHOMENOS (Mantineias):** The Classical and Hellenistic fortified city of Orchomenos lies on the hill above the village of Orchomenos (formerly Kalpaki), north of Levidi. By Pausanias' day this upper city was in ruins though the area around the modern village was inhabited. Dodwell described the site and dug up some Doric capitals in the lower city (Dodwell, *Tour* 2, 1819, 424ff) (cf. Frazer, *Pausanias* 4, 224ff).

The site was visited and planned by H. Latterman in 1910 (F. Hiller von Gärtringen and H. Latterman, *Arkadische Forschungen,* Berlin 1911, 18ff) and the French School under G. Blum and A. Plassart excavated in 1913. In the upper city they uncovered the agora, a temple of Artemis and the theatre. In the lower city they found a number of small baths, probably belonging to private houses of the Roman period. Evidence was found of much earlier habitation at the foot of the Classical city, including Geometric sherds and fragments of Archaic figurines. The temple from which Dodwell's capitals came was excavated. It is a Doric temple probably of the late 6th century (*BCH* 1914, 71ff; 447ff). MH and Mycenaean sherds have been reported from the hill (*Gazetteer* no. 85) (Howell no. 5).

**PALAIOKASTRO (Gortynias):** To the west of the village of Palaiokastro, west of ancient Gortys, is an ancient fortification which is probably the site of Bouphagion. It has been described by E. Meyer (Meyer 1939, 103ff), and P. Charneux and R. Ginouvès examined it in 1955 and 1956. In addition to Classical and later remains, Mycenaean walls and sherds were identified (*BCH* 1956, 522ff). Kh. Khristou in 1957 excavated several Mycenaean chamber tombs at 'Palaiopyrgos', to the west, at least one of which was 'tholos-shaped', and noted traces of many others. A number of LH IIIC vases were recovered and some bronze weapons. A vast cemetery, probably of Roman date, was noted at 'Marmara' (*BCH* 1958, 717) (*AAA* 2, 1969, 226ff) (Howell no. 55).

**PALAIOKHORI (Kynourias):** Mycenaean tombs have been excavated near Palaiokhori, west of Leonidi, though apparently only one group of vases, ranging from LH I/IIA–LH IIIA was ever published (*AD* 9, 1924–25, *par.* 18ff) (*BSA* 56, 1961, 132ff).

**PALLANTION (Mantineias):** The Italian School under A. De Franciscis and G. Libertini excavated at the site of ancient Pallantion, south of modern Tripolis, in 1940. They uncovered part of the acropolis wall, three small Archaic temples on the acropolis, and one below it. To the east of the acropolis two pithos burials and some probable MH pottery were found (*Ann.* 17-18, 1939–40, 225ff) (Howell no. 34).

**TEGEA (Mantineias):** The site of ancient Tegea lies to the southeast of modern Tripolis. A temple of Demeter and Kore was excavated at Ayios Sostis outside the city circuit, in 1860. Primitive bronze and terracotta figurines, probably Geometric and Archaic, were recovered (*Gazette Archéologique* 4, 1878, 42ff) (Frazer, *Pausanias* 4, 440-41). It has since been re-examined by K. Romaios (*PAE* 1909, 316) (*Mikra Meletimata* 1955, 14ff).

In 1888–89, V. Bérard and G. Fougères of the French School investigated the ancient city. They uncovered the agora, a stadium, theatre, a number of inscriptions, and examined the city walls (*BCH* 1892, 329ff; 1893, 1ff).

The temple of Alea Athena had been examined by A. Milchhöfer in 1879 (*AM.* 5, 1880, 52ff) and by W. Dörpfeld in 1882 (*AM* 8, 1883, 274). It was excavated by the French School with G. Mendel, C. Dugas and others in 1900 and 1910. An early shrine was burnt in 392 B.C. and the present temple was then built. Fragments of sculptures by Scopas were recovered. Beneath the temple much earlier material was found: some Mycenaean sherds (LH IIIB–C), an LH IIIB 'psi' figurine, proto-Geometric, Geometric and Archaic sherds, and Geometric and Archaic bronzes (*BCH* 1901, 241ff; 1921, 335ff on material earlier than the 4th century) (C. Dugas, J. Berchmans, M. Clemmensen, *Le Sanctuaire d'Aléa Athéna*, Paris 1924) (*Gazetteer* no. 89) (Howell no. 26).

Fragments of the temple of Alea Athena, including fragments of the pediment sculptures and of a Nike acroterion, were recovered by K. Dimakopoulou in the excavation of a late Roman house in 1964–65 (*AD* 20, 1965, *Chr.* 1, 169f; 21, 1966, *Chr.* 1, 152ff). During the reorganization of the Tegea museum further sculptures were recognized as part of the pediments and acroteria of the temple (*AAA* 1, 1968, 117ff).

**THELPOUSA (Gortynias):** The site of ancient Thelpousa is at 'Vanaina' above Toubitsi on the Ladon. For earlier bibliography and descriptions, see Frazer (Frazer, *Pausanias* 4, 285ff) and E. Meyer (Meyer 1939, 86ff). J. Roger and H. Metzger carried out some soundings in 1938, particularly in the agora, where they uncovered the remains of porticos, perhaps of the 4th century B.C., and an edifice in the middle, perhaps a Roman temple (*BCH* 1939, 301).

**THISOA (Gortynias):** The site of Thisoa is at 'Palaiokatina' near Karkalou, northeast of Dimitsana. The site was described by Latterman (F. Hiller von Gärtringen and H. Latterman, *Arkadische Forschungen*, Berlin 1911, 25 and 37ff) and was partially excavated by G. Oikonomos in 1911. There are remains of the acropolis fortifications, a Hellenistic temple of 'Megas Theos', and late Roman buildings (*PAE* 1911, 243f).

**THOKNIA (Megalopoleos):** The site of ancient Thoknia, deserted in Pausanias' day, is probably near modern Thoknia, formerly Vromosella, near the junction of the Helisson and Alpheios rivers. K. Stephanos carried out some excavation here in 1907 but found only fragments of pottery (*PAE* 1907, 122).

**TRIPOTAMIA (Gortynias):** In 1963 N. and J. Chavaillon found Paleo-lithic implements east of the Erymanthos near the road from Vasiliki in Elis (*BCH* 1964, 616ff).

**VAKHLIA (Gortynias):** In 1891 V. Leonardos excavated several sites in the region of the upper Ladon. On the acropolis 'Ston arte' at Vakhlia he uncovered the foundation of a small temple (*AD* 1891, 99-100). For a de-scription of the region, see Frazer (Frazer, *Pausanias* 4, 289ff). See also Dimitra and Voutsi (cf. *AE* 1965, *Chr.* 6ff). In 1937 at Palaiokastro, a ridge about one km southwest of the village, E. Meyer found traces of Classi-cal and Hellenistic occupation, and an obsidian arrowhead. This is per-haps the site of Thaliades mentioned by Pausanias (VIII 25.2) (Meyer 1939, 71ff). Kh. Khristou reported Classical tombs discovered by vil-lagers somewhere in the vicinity, and a Geometric bronze statuette of a bull (*BCH* 1960, 693).

**VLAKHORRAPTI (Gortynias):** P. Charneux and R. Ginouvès examined the fortress of Ayios Nikolaos overlooking this village, west of ancient Gortys, which they dated to the 4th or 3rd century B.C. (*BCH* 1956, 538ff).

**VOUTSI (Gortynias):** In 1891 V. Leonardos excavated several sites in the region of the upper Ladon. At Voutsi he uncovered the foundations of a small building, perhaps a temple (*AD* 1891, 100) (*PAE* 1891, 23ff). In 1938 J. Roger and H. Metzger conducted soundings at some of the many ruined churches in the village. Under the Ayia Marina chapel they found part of a building, perhaps the temple of Asclepios mentioned by Pausa-nias (VIII 25.1) (*BCH* 1939, 301).

V. Leonardos reported antiquities from a place called Kleivoka some-where south of Kontovazaina, northeast of Voutsi (*AD* 1891, 98). Miss Kh. Kardara discovered a temple foundation nearby (*Ergon* 1966, 102ff) (*PAE* 1966, 115f) (*AE* 1965, *Chr.* 9f).

**VOUVOURA (Kynourias):** Prehistoric remains were discovered on the Analipsis hill about 4 km west of Vouvoura in 1900 (*AE* 1900, 90). K. Ro-maios has excavated the site beginning in 1950 for the Greek Archaeological Society. A town of the Classical period has been partially uncovered, probably ancient Iasos which was destroyed in 147 B.C. Houses, a defense wall, and a building which is perhaps a shrine were excavated. A large amount of red-figure pottery, probably from a local factory, was recovered. Below the Classical layer Mycenaean sherds and a Mycenaean cist burial were found, and some Geometric sherds, but no buildings have been identified. In 1954 Romaios excavated a large collapsed Mycenaean tholos tomb to the west of the hill and in 1956–57 a group of small tholoi. Bronze swords and terracotta figurines were among the finds (*PAE* for years 1950, 1954 through 1958, and 1961) (*Ergon* 1954, 38-39, 1956, 81ff; 1957, 66ff; 1961, 162ff) (*BSA* 1961, 130) (Howell no. 36).

# Argolid

**ALEA:** E. Meyer visited and described the site of the fortified town of Alea, 4 km south of modern Alea (formerly Bougiati) in the northwest Argolid (Meyer 1939, 19ff). N. Verdelis investigated the site in 1963 in an attempt to locate the sanctuaries mentioned by Pausanias (VIII 23.1) and uncovered part of a Roman building (*AD* 19, 1964, *Chr.* 1, 127).

**ARGOS:** Modern Argos partly occupied the site of the ancient city. For early bibliography see Frazer (Frazer, *Pausanias* 3, 189ff). The theatre was partly excavated by I. Kophiniotis in 1891 (*AD* 1891, 86) (*AM* 16, 1891, 383).

The French School under C. W. Vollgraff excavated at various times between 1902 and 1930 in areas not covered by the modern city, including on the Aspis or Ayios Elias hill, the Deiras ridge area between the Aspis and the Larissa or Kastro, the city walls, and the agora area. An early Bronze Age settlement was found on the Aspis, and 6th century B.C. fortification walls on prehistoric foundations. On the Deiras a Mycenaean cemetery was discovered (*BCH* 1904, 364ff; 1906, 5ff; 1907, 139ff; 1920, 219ff; 1928, 476ff; 1930, 480ff) (*Mnemosyne* 56, 1928, 313ff).

Excavations were resumed in 1952 with G. Roux, P. Courbin and P. Charneux, and work has continued since. Others taking part have included C. W. Vollgraff, R. Ginouvès, J. Deshayes, B. Groslier, Y. Garlan, F. Croissant, J. R. Bommelaer, J. P. Sodini, H. Sarian and P. Aupert. The area around the agora and between the agora and the Larissa was excavated. An originally 5th century B.C. stoa was uncovered, and the Ro-

man Odeion, where Vollgraff had done some work, was excavated. To
the west of the agora a cemetery ranging from the MH period to Roman
times with particularly important proto-Geometric and Geometric burials was excavated. More clearance work was done in the theatre. At the
foot of the Larissa and southeast of the Odeion various excavations were
made. Proto-Geometric and Geometric tombs were found, a Geometric
workshop and potter's kiln, and Hellenistic cist graves. LH IIIC material
was found, and an MH cremation trench. Over an area of MH habitation
the remains of an Aphrodision were discovered. Votive material, some
with inscriptions to Aphrodite, ranging from Archaic to Roman times,
was recovered, and the foundations of a probably 5th century B.C. temple uncovered. The fortifications of the Larissa were studied. The Mycenaean cemetery on the Deiras was further excavated. It was in use at
least from the LH II period, in LH IIIA–B, and possibly into the sub-
Mycenaean period. More than 35 chamber tombs and 25 pit graves were
excavated. The area of the Sanctuary of Apollo and Athena between the
Deiras cemetery and the Aspis was explored. In the city, around the
new museum, a proto-Geometric to Archaic cemetery with cist and
pithos burials was excavated. In 1974, work was resumed on the Aspis for
the first time since 1904. MH material was recovered, and some probably
late Neolithic. Preliminary reports have been published annually in *BCH*
since 1958. The following publications have also appeared:

> C. W. Vollgraff, *Le sanctuaire d'Apollon pythéen d'Argos,* École fran-
> çaise d'Athènes, *Études péloponnésiennes* I, Paris 1956.
> J. Deshayes, *Argos, les fouilles de la Deiras, Études péloponnésiennes* IV,
> Paris 1966.
> R. Ginouvès, *Le théâtron à gradins droits et l'odéon, Études péloponnési-
> ennes* VI, Paris 1972.
> P. Courbin, *Tombes géometriques d'Argos I (1952–1958), Études pélo-
> ponnésiennes* VIII, Paris 1974.

The Greek Archaeological Service has conducted rescue excavations
in the area of the modern city, reported in the *Chronika* sections of *AD*
annually since 1960. Some of the more important are: six Geometric cist
graves in George II Street (*AD* 18, 1963, *Chr.* 1, 57ff); six sub-Mycenaean
graves and 37 Classical and Hellenistic graves in Tripolis Street south of
the theatre (ibid., 60ff), a Classical and Hellenistic cemetery on the site of
the Gymnasterion (*AD* 19, 1964, *Chr.* 1, 122ff; 22, 1967, *Chr.* 1, 169ff),
various MH burials including a MH tumulus, and transitional MH
III/LH I cist graves, two Mycenaean chamber tombs from the Deiras,
and a Geometric cist tomb (*AD* 26, 1971, *Chr.* 1, 74ff). On Argos, the following publications have also appeared (Scoufopoulos 29, 33ff) (*Archae-*

*ology* 9, 1956, 166ff: summary of site) (Ålin 42f) (Desborough 80ff) (R. Hägg, *Die Gräber der Argolis 1*, Uppsala 1974) (R. A. Tomlinson, *Argos and the Argolid*, London 1972: post Bronze Age Argolid).


**ARIA:** From Aria, east of Nauplion, Mycenaean chamber tombs with LH II–IIIA vases have been reported (*BCH* 1955, 244).


**ASINE:** The French School did some preliminary mapping of the acropolis of Asine in 1920 (*BCH* 1921, 295) and in 1922, 1924, 1926 and 1928 the Swedish Institute under A. Persson excavated at Asine. In 1922 the then Prince, Gustaf Adolf, took part. On the acropolis remains of EH to LH IIIC2 habitation were found, remains of EH houses and a storage pit, MH burials, and LH houses. One LH IIIC house included a shrine. The Mycenaean remains peter out without any evidence of destruction. Some poor walls attest proto-Geometric and Geometric occupation, and a deposit of Archaic terracotta figurines was found. A lower town, occupied in the Bronze Age, was also partly excavated, and two Mycenaean cemeteries on the slopes of Mt. Barbouna opposite Asine to the north. Little LH IIIB material was recovered from the graves, but over 80 LH IIIC vases. Preliminary reports: (*Bull. Lund* 1922–23, 25ff; 1923–24, 162ff; 1924–25, 23ff). Final report: (O. Frödin and A. W. Persson, *Asine, Results of the Swedish Excavations 1922–1930*, Stockholm 1938). Also: (R. Hägg, "Geometrische Gräber von Asine," *Op. Ath.* 6, 1965, 117ff) (P. Ålin, "Unpublished Sherds from Asine," *Op. Ath.* 8, 1968, 87ff) (cf. Scoufopoulos 30, 56ff) (Desborough 82ff) (M. P. Nilsson, "A House Sanctuary at Asine," in *The Minoan-Mycenaean Religion and its Survival in Greek Religion*, 2nd ed., Lund 1950, 110ff).

The site was severely plundered for stone by the Italians during the war (*BCH* 1944–45, 428). A Geometric bronze female figurine has been found on the acropolis (*AE* 1953, 318ff). A 5th century cist tomb was excavated northwest of the acropolis by I. Papachristodoulou (*AD* 23, 1968, *Chr.* 1, 132ff). E. Protonotariou-Deilaki has reported on excavations on building plots east of the acropolis in 1969. Finds included an MH cist grave and part of a Mycenaean house (*AD* 25, 1970, *Chr.* 1, 157ff).

In 1970 the Swedish Institute under C.-G. Styrenius resumed excavations which have continued since. East of the acropolis above the beach an MH cist grave cemetery, part of an MH tumulus, Mycenaean material including LH IIIC and sub-Mycenaean pottery, and proto-Geometric and Geometric settlement remains were found. R. and I. Hägg have been excavating on the Barbouna hill. MH material, remains of Mycenaean buildings with LH II–IIIA pottery and of a late Geometric settlement were uncovered. An MH shaft grave was found cut into bedrock (*AAA* 4, 1971, 147ff) (*AR* 1970–71, 11; 1971–72, 9; 1972–73, 14f; 1973–74, 11; 1974–75, 10) (R. and I. Hägg, ed., *Excavation in the Barbouna Area at Asine*, Uppsala 1973).

A recent survey article related to the Bronze Age cemetery by Dietz has appeared (*Archaeology* 28, 3, 1975, 157ff).

**AYIOS ADRIANOS:** In a trial excavation in 1962 E. Protonotariou-Deilaki discovered an Archaic votive deposit by the chapel of Profitis Elias on a hill northwest of the village. The chapel rests on a temple foundation. Remains of a Mycenaean settlement were found below the votive deposit and traces of Cyclopean walls surround the hill. Remains of an ancient town, perhaps Lessa (Pausanias II 25.9) were noted below the hill (*AD* 18, 1963, *Chr.* 1, 65ff) (*BCH* 1963, 748) (*Gazetteer* no. 11).

**DENDRA:** In 1926 the Swedish Institute under A. Persson in conjunction with the Greek Department of Antiquities excavated an unplundered tholos tomb at Dendra near the acropolis of Midea. In one pit were the skeletons of a man and a woman, the 'King and Queen', in another a girl; two other pits were perhaps disturbed in antiquity. Rich finds including gold and silver cups, weapons and LH IIIA pottery were recovered. In 1927, 1937, and 1939 Persson excavated a number of Mycenaean chamber tombs with LH II–IIIB finds (A. W. Persson, *The Royal Tombs at Dendra near Midea*, Lund 1931; A. W. Persson, *New Tombs at Dendra near Midea*, Lund 1942). In 1956 N. Verdelis discovered another tholos tomb (tomb no. 12) which Verdelis and P. Åström excavated in 1960. The tomb had been partly wrecked in the meantime. There had been only one burial. Vases of LH IIB–IIIA date were recovered, and a set of bronze armour, a corselet, fragments of greaves, and boars' tusks and bronze cheek pieces from a helmet. Another tholos (tomb no. 13) was also excavated. The remains were mostly LH IIIA date with the latest burial being of LH IIIB date (*AD* 16, 1960, *Chr.* 93ff) (*AE* 1957, *Chr.* 15ff) (*Praktika tis Akadimias Athinon* 37, 1962, 72ff). Another chamber tomb was excavated in 1962 (*AD* 18, 1963, *Chr.* 1, 63ff).

Persson had carried out some trials on the acropolis of Midea, east of the cemetery, in 1939 (cf. *Op. Ath.* 7, 1967, 161ff). In 1961–63 and in 1965 it was explored by R. Hägg and P. Åström (*Op. Ath.* 4, 1964, 86ff; 5,

1965, 79ff). (*AD* 19, 1964, *Chr.* 1, 134). It was occupied throughout the Bronze Age and the Cyclopean walls survive. Next to Gla, it is the largest Mycenaean fortress in extent (Scoufopoulos 54ff) (*Gazetteer* nos. 6-7) (Ålin 40ff).

**ELIOKASTRO:** Eliokastro, northeast of Kranidi, is probably the site of ancient Eileoi. There are extensive remains of circuit walls. A. Philadelpheus found a number of Mycenaean cist tombs in 1909 (*PAE* 1909, 182ff) (Ålin 52) (*Gazetteer* no. 32).

**EPIDAUROS:** P. Kavvadias and V. Stais excavated at the sanctuary at Epidauros beginning in 1881, uncovering the theatre, various temples, the gymnasium, and associated buildings in the sanctuary area. Kavvadias continued to work at the site, making it his life work (P. Kavvadias, *Fouilles de Épidaure I,* Athens 1893) (P. Kavvadias, *To ieron tou Asklipiou en Epidauro,* Athens 1900) (*PAE* for years 1881–87, 1891–96, 1898–1907, 1916, 1918–27).

R. Martin and H. Metzger investigated parts of the site including the temple of Asclepios in 1945 (*BCH* 1946, 352ff). Between 1948 and 1951 I. Papadimitriou worked at the site, but concentrated mainly on the temple of Apollo Maleatas on the heights east of the sanctuary. Most of the finds were of the Archaic period. The temple dates from the mid-fourth century; previously there was perhaps only an altar. Beneath the sanctuary a great deal of prehistoric material dating back to the EH period was found. LH III remains, human and animal figurines, indicate that there was a cult here also in the Mycenaean period. Although Papadimitriou claimed that there was a probable continuity of cult into the historic period, there have been apparently no finds after the LH IIIB period until the 7th century (*PAE* 1948, 90f; 1949, 91ff; 1950, 194ff; 1951, 204ff) (Desborough 42f, 78). V. Lambrinoudakis and M. Mitsos resumed work on the site in 1974. Fragmentary remains of the pedimental sculptures were recovered (*Ergon* 1974, 57ff) (*AR* 1974–75, 10). On the Sanctuary at Epidauros, see also: (A. von Gerkan and W. Müller-Wiener, *Das Theater von Epidauros,* Paris 1961) (A. Burford, *The Greek Temple Builders at Epidauros,* Liverpool 1969).

**Palaia Epidauros:** The site of the ancient city of Epidauros has been described by Frazer (Frazer, *Pausanias* 3, 259ff). There are remains of fortification walls, and the ruins of a small temple. In 1888 V. Stais excavated seven Mycenaean chamber tombs near the harbour (*AD* 1888, 155ff). I. Papadimitriou investigated the site and described various remains (*PAE* 1951, 204ff). E. Protonotariou-Deilaki excavated the theatre in 1970 (*AD* 26, 1971, *Chr.* 1, 84) (*AAA* 5, 1972, 347ff). K. Kritzas and J. Whittlesey surveyed underwater remains (*AAA* 5, 1972, 186ff). A necropolis of Geometric to Roman times has been discovered at 'Minia' about 1.5 km from the city (*AD* 23, 1968, 133).

**Nea Epidauros:** Mycenaean chamber tombs were reported at 'Dimena' or 'Vassa' inland from Nea Epidauros and an MH and LH II–IIIB settlement with some Cyclopean walls was noted (*AA* 1938, 559ff) (Ålin 52) (*Gazetteer* nos. 24-5). (On the area of Epidauros, see: N. Faraklas, *Epidauria, Ancient Greek Cities* no. 12, Athens Technological Organization, Athens Center of Ekistics, Athens 1972.)

**GYMNO:** J. F. Lazenby and R. Hope Simpson discovered a Mycenaean settlement on the Kastro hill about 3 km southeast of the village. A few gray Minyan sherds and copious LH II–IIIB sherds were noted as well as remains of a probably Classical watch tower (*Gazetteer* no. 18).

**HERAION:** The site of the Argive Heraion was discovered by chance in 1831 by General Gordon of Cairness. He carried out some small excavations in 1836. In 1854 Rangabé and Bursian partly uncovered the foundations of the later temple (C. Bursian, *Bulletino dell' Instituto di Corrisp. Archeol.* 1854, xiii-xvii). The American School under C. Waldstein carried out large scale excavations from 1892 to 1895, the first major project of the school. On the upper terrace part of the old temple of the early 7th century was excavated. Its upper structure may have been mud brick and wood, as little survives. The new temple, a late 5th century Doric building, stands on a lower terrace surrounded by stoas and other buildings, including a small late 7th century building and a 6th century stoa. To the west, baths and a palaestra were excavated. Fragments of metopes and pediment sculptures were recovered as well as votives and other material going back to the late Geometric period. Waldstein also discovered remains of a prehistoric settlement and some Mycenaean tombs north of the south stoa, and two tholos shaped chamber tombs to the northwest of the sanctuary. P. Stamatakis had previously excavated a beehive tomb in 1878 (*PAE* 1878, 17) (*AM* 3, 1878, 271ff) (C. Waldstein, *Excavations of the American School of Athens at the Heraion of Argos I,*

London 1892) (C. Waldstein et al., *The Argive Heraion*, 2 vols., Boston 1902). For a summary of these excavations and the earlier explorations see also Frazer (Frazer, *Pausanias* 3, 165ff).

From 1925–28 C. Blegen excavated the prehistoric remains at the site. EH remains including walls were found on the hill above the old temple beneath disturbed MH and LH material. To the northwest he discovered a burnt Neolithic deposit. To the north and northwest of the sanctuary Neolithic and EH burials were uncovered, MH cist graves and a series of over 50 Mycenaean chamber tombs, the latest burials being LH IIIB (*AE* 1937, 377ff) (C. W. Blegen, *Prosymna: The Helladic Settlement Preceding the Argive Heraion*, Cambridge 1937).

J. Caskey of the American School and P. Amandry of the French School excavated in the sanctuary area in 1949. They uncovered an Archaic deposit of over 900 miniature vases, some bronze phialai and terracottas. They also found prehistoric material; some of the sherds may be early LH IIIC (*Hesperia* 21, 1952, 165ff). In 1957 N. Verdelis excavated another Mycenaean chamber tomb, with mostly LH IIIA–B remains, but the tomb was in use from the LH II period to possibly LH IIIC (*AE* 1956, *par.* 10ff) (*AE* 1960, 123ff). Another LH IIIA–B chamber tomb was excavated in 1969 (*AD* 25, 1970, *Chr.* 1, 156) (cf. Desborough 77f) (Ålin 37ff) (*Gazetteer* no. 4).

**HERMIONI:** Ancient Hermioni lay on the promontory east of the modern village. For bibliography of early travellers, see Frazer (Frazer, *Pausanias* 3, 293ff). A. Philadelpheus investigated the site in 1909, exploring the remains of a temple of Poseidon on the promontory, and the ancient cemetery. Philadelpheus also reported Mycenaean sherds (*PAE* 1909, 172ff) (cf. *Gazetteer* no. 31). The site has also been explored and described by A. Frickenhaus and W. Müller (*AM* 36, 1911, 37) and by M. Jameson (*Hesperia* 28, 1959, 109ff). M. McAllister has studied the remains of the Poseidon temple, dated probably to the late 6th century (*Hesperia* 38, 1969, 169ff). (See also N. Faraklas, *Hermionis-Halias, Ancient Greek Cities no. 19*, Athens Center of Ekistics, Athens 1973; in modern Greek.)

**IRIA:** In 1939 K. Gebauer excavated a Mycenaean house on the Kastro tou Kapetanou by Iria, southeast of Asine. There were two levels, one with a great deal of LH IIIB pottery, and the other with some early LH IIIC (*AA* 1939, 287ff) (*Tiryns VI*, Mainz 1974, 57ff).

**KANDIA:** In 1939 K. Gebauer excavated on the fortified hill at Kandia, east of Asine. Part of an apsidal EH house, MH and LH walls and Mycenaean fortifications, as well as Roman buildings, were discovered on the acropolis. In a lower town some Mycenaean houses were excavated, with MH walls and some EH pottery beneath them (*AA* 1939, 288ff) (*Neue Jahrbücher für Antike und deutsche Bildung* 1940, 18ff) (Ålin 49ff) (*Gazetteer* no. 26) (Scoufopoulos 56).

On the Synoro hill northwest of Kandia Gebauer partly excavated a mainly EH prehistoric site. EH I 'sauceboats' were recovered (AA 1939, 288ff) (*Tiryns VI*, Mainz 1974, 79ff) (Ålin 50) (*Gazetteer* no. 27).

**KAZARMA:** At Kazarma, about 8 km west of Lygourio on the Nauplion-Epidauros road, MH, LH IIIA–B remains and Classical or Hellenistic fortifications have been noted. There is a probably Mycenaean bridge at Arkadiko (*BCH* 1955, 244ff) (*Gazetteer* no. 20). A tholos tomb, noted by S. Kharitonidis in 1966 (*AD* 22, 1967, *Chr.* 1, 179f) was excavated by E. Protonotariou-Deilaki and S. Marinatos in 1969. Three pits in the floor contained burials and rich offerings including a gold diadem. LH I–II vases were recovered. The tomb continued in use until early LH IIIC (*AAA* 1, 1968, 236ff; 2, 1969, 3ff) (*AD* 24, 1969, *Chr.* 1, 164f).

**KEPHALARI CAVE:** Upper Paleolithic and later deposits were recovered from the Kephalari Cave 8 km south of Argos by R. C. S. Felsch (*AAA* 6, 1973, 13ff) (*AR* 1972–73, 15).

**KIVERI:** About 5 km southwest of Kiveri (south of Myloi), and about 2 km south of Spiliotaki station, the remains of a small temple were excavated in 1963. Votives from the late 6th to the late 4th century B.C. including terracotta female figurines were recovered (*AD* 19, 1964, *Chr.* 1, 121ff).

In 1966 seven Mycenaean chamber tombs of LH IIIA–B date were excavated by K. Krystalli by the Kiveri cemetery, and the remains of a Roman quarry were noted (*AD* 22, 1967, *Chr.* 1, 179f).

**KOILADA:** A Mycenaean settlement with LH IIIB sherds, and a Classical and Hellenistic fort have been noted on the Ayios Ioannis promontory 2 km north of the village (*Klio*, Beiheft 49, 1944, 48-49) (Ålin 52) (*Gazetteer* no. 29).

For the Franchthi Cave see Porto Kheli.

**KOURTAKI:** In 1966–67 and 1969 at Kourtaki, about 8 km east of Argos, late 7th century vases and various terracotta figurines were found in an excavation of a building, perhaps a workshop (*AD* 22, 1967, *Chr.* 1, 178f; 23, 1968, *Chr.* 1, 131f; 25, 1970, *Chr.* 1, 155f).

**LERNA:** Between 1952 and 1958 J. Caskey of the American School excavated a prehistoric site by Myloi village (ancient Lerna). The site had been discovered by A. Frickenhaus and W. Müller in 1909 (*AM* 36, 1911, 24). The site was occupied from the Neolithic to the LH IIIB period, the EH and MH remains being the most important. Neolithic graves and house remains were discovered, a massive EH fortification wall, and a large EH I building, replaced by the larger 'House of Tiles' (25 m by 12 m) which was itself destroyed by fire at the end of EH II (Lerna III). The EH III settlement continued without any violent break into the MH period. MH apsidal houses, repeatedly rebuilt, and MH cist graves and simple interments were uncovered. In the middle of the mound a transitional MH/LH I shaft grave was excavated, and LH III houses were found on the site (*Hesperia* 23, 1954, 3ff; 24, 1955, 25ff; 25, 1956, 147ff; 26, 1957, 142ff; 27, 1958, 125ff; 28, 1959, 202ff; 29, 1960, 285ff). Final publications have begun to appear (N.-G. Gejvall, *Lerna I, The Fauna*, Princeton 1969; J. L. Angel, *Lerna II, The People*, Princeton 1971).

In 1956 E. Protonotariou-Deilaki excavated two slab covered rectangular LH I–II tombs at Myloi, and noted Classical tombs (*AE* 1955, *par.* 1ff). About 2 km south of Myloi N. Verdelis excavated three plundered Mycenaean chamber tombs in 1957. LH IIIB vases were recovered (*AE* 1956, *par.* 12ff). In 1966 eight transitional MH/LH I graves were excavated by S. Kharitonidis (*AD* 22, 1967, *Chr.* 1, 182). Another was excavated in 1970 (*AD* 26, 1971, *Chr.* 1, 83).

**MAZI:** Remains of Classical buildings have been partially excavated at Mazi, perhaps ancient Oinoe (*AD* 26, 1971, *Chr.* 1, 84).

**METHANA:** For various antiquities noted on the Methana peninsula, see Frazer (Frazer, *Pausanias* 3, 286ff), M. Deffner (*AM* 34, 1909, 341ff) and N. Faraklas (*AGC* no. 10).

**MONASTERAKI:** In 1919–20 A. Philadelpheus excavated five LH III chamber tombs at Priftani (now renamed Monasteraki) south of Mycenae (*AD* 5, 1919, *par.* 34ff) and S. Kharitonidis excavated two more about 1950, and noted traces of a prehistoric settlement on the Magoula hill on the southwest side of the village (*AE* 1952, *par.* 19ff) (Ålin 37) (*Gazetteer* no. 2).

**MYCENAE:** The location of Mycenae has always been known, and travellers, ancient and modern, have commented on the ruins. Lord Elgin explored the 'Treasury of Atreus' in 1802, and Lord Sligo removed the columns from it in 1910 which are now in the British Museum (cf. *JHS* 36, 1916, 213f). In 1840 K. Pittakis of the Greek Archaeological Society cleared the Lion Gate and outer court (*PAE* 1840–41, 136ff). H. Schliemann was the first to carry out substantial excavation. He tested the site in 1874, and in 1876 excavated most of 'Grave Circle A' within the fortifications and discovered the famous gold treasures. He also made small excavations within the citadel. Mrs. Schliemann partly excavated the tholos known as the 'Tomb of Clytemnestra' (H. Schliemann, *Mycenae: A Narrative of Researches and Discoveries at Mycenae and Tiryns*, N.Y. 1880) (C. Schuchhardt, *Schliemann's Excavations*, London 1891, 134ff). P. Stamatakis continued Schliemann's work, finding a sixth shaft grave in the grave circle and clearing the 'Treasury of Atreus' (*PAE* 1876, 12ff; 1877, 24ff; 1878, 16f).

In 1886 Kh. Tsountas began his important series of excavations which lasted into this century. He cleared much of the citadel and palace, various houses on the citadel and over 70 chamber tombs in the cemetery. He also examined the later temple built on the site (*PAE* for years 1886, 1888, 1890, 1892, 1893) (*AE* for years 1887, 1888, 1891, 1897, 1902) (Kh. Tsountas, *Mykinai kai Mykinaios Politismos*, Athens 1893, translated as *The Mycenaean Age*, London 1897). On all these 19th century excavations, see Frazer (Frazer, *Pausanias* 3, 94ff).

D. Evangelidis excavated a cemetery of the Geometric town in 1909 (*AE* 1912, 127ff). The next large scale excavation was that of the British School under A. J. B. Wace in 1920–23. Work was carried out chiefly in the palace area, but the entire site was re-examined, the 'Tomb of Aegisthus' was cleared and the Hellenistic lower town partly excavated. Among those also taking part were C. Blegen and W. Lamb (*BSA* 24, 1919–21, 185ff; 25, 1921–23, 1ff). Chamber tombs have also been excavated by A. Philadelpheus and M. Mitsos (A. J. B. Wace, "Chamber Tombs at Mycenae," *Archaeologia* 82, 1932, 1ff).

Wace resumed his pre-war excavation in 1950 and work continued until 1957. The prehistoric cemetery on both sides of the fortification wall of which Grave Circle A was part was examined. Many MH graves and some LH IIIC and Geometric graves were excavated. Several houses within the citadel and outside it were excavated; 'Tsountas' House' was re-examined, and excavation was begun on the 'Citadel House', or 'Wace's House'. The 'House of the Oil Merchant', the 'House of the Wine Merchant', the 'House of Shields', and the 'House of Sphinxes' were other buildings excavated. Supplementary excavations were carried out in the palace (*BSA* 48, 1953, 3ff; 49, 1954, 231ff; 50, 1955, 173ff; 51, 1956, 103ff; 52, 1957, 193ff).

At the same time the Greek Archaeological Society and the Greek Department of Antiquities have been working on the site in various areas in and around the citadel. In 1951 'Grave Circle B' was discovered outside the citadel. It dates from the MH III period and was partly destroyed when the 'Tomb of Clytemnestra' was built. I. Papadimitriou with G. Mylonas and D. Theocharis excavated the circle between 1952 and 1954. Very rich probably royal graves were uncovered, the latest being of the LH I period (*PAE* for years 1950 through 1954) (G. E. Mylonas, *Grave Circle B of Mycenae, Studies in Mediterranean Archaeology* no. 7, Lund 1964) (G. E. Mylonas, *O Taphikos Kyklos B ton Mykinon,* 2 vols., Athens 1972–73).

In 1957 N. Verdelis began excavation in the 'West House' discovered behind the House of the Oil Merchant. Linear B tablets were discovered. The house is slightly older than the House of the Oil Merchant; they were destroyed by fire at the same time at the end of LH IIIB. Excavation in and around this house continued through 1962. The entrance to the House of the Oil Merchant was located, and a small Geometric apsidal building which Verdelis suggests is a temple was excavated. Mrs. Wace French also worked in this area in 1961 in the House of Sphinxes and the House of the Oil Merchant (*AD* 17, 1961–62, *Chr.* 64ff) (*PAE* for years 1957 through 1962).

G. Mylonas began a series of excavations in 1958 which have continued to the present. He worked in various areas both inside the citadel and outside. He studied the gates and walls of the fortress (*AE* 1958, 153ff; 1962, 1ff), excavated houses to the north of the Treasury of Atreus, worked on the northwest and east slopes within the citadel, and recently in the area around Tsountas' House. He also excavated four LH IIIC chamber tombs at 'Gortsoulia' about 2 km to the northeast in 1964 (*AD* 20, 1965, *Chr.* 1, 160ff) and LH IIIB tombs at 'Vlachostrata' and 'Kapsala' also to the northeast in 1972. S. Iakovidis has worked with Mylonas in recent years. His work has been reported annually in *PAE* and *Ergon,* and in *AR* and *BCH* (cf. *Hesperia* 35, 1966, 419ff).

Lord William Taylour, first with I. Papadimitriou (1959–60, 1962) and then under Mylonas' supervision (1964, 1968–69) completed the excavation of the Citadel House begun by Wace. One room had had a frescoed mural; another, with benches around it, had been a shrine. The house was partly rebuilt and reoccupied in the LH IIIC period. This area of the acropolis may have been of sacred use. Mylonas recently has discovered an altar and other LH IIIB cult remains in the area of the Tsountas' House (*Antiquity* 35, 1961, 57f; 43, 1969, 91ff; 44, 1970, 270ff) (*ILN* Jan. 4, 1969; Dec. 27, 1969; Jan. 10, 1970) (*BSA* 68, 1973, 87ff) (*AD* 16, 1960, *Chr.* 89ff; 18, 1963, *Chr.* 1, 82ff; 20, 1965, *Chr.* 1, 164ff) (*AR* 1960, 30ff; 1962–63, 13ff; 1964–65, 11ff; 1966–67, 8f; 1968–69, 11ff; 1969–70, 11ff).

Leslie Shear Jr., under Mylonas' supervision, excavated a small Archaic to Hellenistic sanctuary, apparently dedicated to Enyalios, at 'Aspra Komata', one km north of the citadel in 1965–66 (*AR* 1965–66, 7; 1966–67, 8).

Among the copious publications on Mycenae, the following might be noted in addition to those mentioned above:

> G. E. Mylonas, *Ancient Mycenae,* 1957.
> G. E. Mylonas, *Mycenae and the Mycenaean Age,* 1966.
> A. Furumark, *Mycenaean Pottery,* 1941, and *The Chronology of Mycenaean Pottery,* 1941.
> S. Marinatos and M. Hirmer, *Crete and Mycenae,* 1960.
> G. Karo, *Die Schachtgräber von Mykenai,* 1930.
> Lord William Taylour, *The Mycenaeans,* 1964.
> R. Hägg, *Die Gräber der Argolis* 1, Uppsala 1974, 64ff.
> Desborough, 73ff.
> Scoufopoulos, 29 and 34ff.

See also the series of articles by E. French on the chronology of Mycenaean pottery (*BSA* 56, 1961; 58, 1963 and 64, 1969) and the *Guide to Mycenae* (prepared by Mrs. Wace and C. Williams, 4th ed., 1966).

**NAUPLION:** The Its-Kale Castle was the ancient acropolis but little which is ancient remains except for blocks reused in the Medieval and modern fortifications. Most of the finds from Nauplion have been from pre-Classical periods. Mycenaean sherds have been reported from the acropolis by A. Frickenhaus and W. Müller (*AM* 36, 1911, 37) and Mycenaean chamber tombs have been excavated on the northeast slopes of the Palamidi fortress by E. Kastorkhis and I. Kondakis with H. Lolling in 1878–80, and by V. Stais in 1892. Over forty tombs were found. A few contained LH IIIC material (*Athenaion* 1878, 183ff; 1879, 517ff) (*PAE* 1878, 17ff; 1880, 21; 1892, 52ff) (*AE* 1895, 261) (*AM* 5, 1880, 143ff). Between 1953 and 1955 S. Kharitonidis worked in this area, extending into the Pronoia suburb. He excavated a few more Mycenaean tombs, Geometric pithos burials, Classical tombs and a Geometric house (*PAE* 1953, 195ff; 1954, 155ff; 1955, 233ff).

A Neolithic and EH settlement was found in Pronoia and partly excavated by E. Protonotariou-Deilaki (*AAA* 4, 1971, 10f) (*AD* 26, 1971, *Chr.* 1, 74).

**PORTO KHELI:** The University of Pennsylvania and the University of Indiana for the American School excavated two sites in the area of Porto Kheli: the site of ancient Halieis opposite the modern village in 1962, 1965–68, 1970–74 and the Franchthi Cave near Koilada in 1967–69, 1971, 1973–74. Work at Halieis was carried out by J. Young, M. Jameson, C. K. Williams, T. W. Jacobsen and W. R. Rudolph. On the acropolis, sherds from the Neolithic to the LH II period have been found. A 7th century mud brick defense wall has been excavated, and a later fortification probably associated with the settlement of the people expelled from Tiryns in the 5th century, also of mud brick. Various buildings were excavated including a small sanctuary area with 5th century votives, a rectangular building, perhaps the Bouleuterion, a dye-works and warehouse, and houses. Remains now submerged in the harbour were surveyed, including a temple, probably of Apollo, with finds from the late Geometric period to the mid 5th century. No remains of after about 330 B.C. were found at the site (*Hesperia* 38, 1969, 311ff; 43, 1974, 105ff) (*AD* 18, 1963, *Chr.* 1, 73ff; 21, 1966, *Chr.* 1, 148ff; 22, 1967, *Chr.* 1, 195f; 23, 1968, *Chr.* 1, 144ff; 24, 1969, *Chr.* 1, 124ff; 26, 1971, *Chr.* 1, 114ff) (*AR* 1971–72, 9f; 1972–73, 15f; 1973–74, 11ff; 1974–75, 10ff).

Work at the Franchthi Cave was directed largely by T. W. Jacobsen of the University of Indiana. There are at least 6 km of cave, and the earliest occupation dates to about 18,000 B.C. There were at least two Paleolithic settlements within the cave. Occupation continued throughout the Mesolithic and Neolithic periods. A new population element seems to have appeared about 6000 B.C. The cave was abandoned near the end of the Neolithic period. A few finds of the historical period indicate that there may have been a cult in the cave. The area outside the cave was also explored. Here occupation begins with the Neolithic period (*Hesperia* 38, 1969, 343ff; 42, 1973, 45ff, 253ff) (*AD* 23, 1968, *Chr.* 1, 144ff; 24, 1969, *Chr.* 1, 124ff; 25, 1970, 169ff) (*AR* 1971–72, 10; 1973–74, 13f; 1974–75, 12). (See also N. Faraklas, *Hermionis-Halias, Ancient Greek Cities* no. 19, Athens Center of Ekistics, Athens 1973; in modern Greek.)

**PROSYMNA:** In excavation reports the area of Argive Heraion is referred to as Prosymna, see Heraion. The present village of Prosymna (formerly Berbati) is about 7 km northeast of the Heraion. In 1935–37 a Swedish expedition under A. Persson excavated on the Kastraki hill, about 2 km west of the village, part of a prehistoric settlement, a complex of LH III houses and a potter's kiln on the east slope, and an EH settlement and an early MH settlement on the south slope. There are also Greek and Roman remains. About one km northwest a tholos tomb with LH II–IIIA remains was excavated, some LH II–IIIB chamber tombs, and an underground chamber of Roman times containing 24 skeletons (G. Säflund, *Excavations at Berbati*, Stockholm 1965). Åkerström returned to the site in 1953 and excavated 12 MH tombs and an LH pottery workshop (*BCH* 1954, 117) (Ålin 38ff) (*Gazetteer* no. 5).

**SKAPHIDAKI:** E. Protonotariou-Deilaki excavated Classical tombs near Skaphidaki in 1961 (*AD* 17, 1961–62, *Chr.* 54).

**SKHINOKHORI:** On the Melkhi or Skala hill between this village in the northwest Argolid and the Inachos River, L. Renaudin excavated five Mycenaean chamber tombs in 1920 and noted a settlement between the tombs and the village. EH, MH, and LH sherds, but nothing later, have been found here (*BCH* 1920, 386ff; 1923, 190ff) (Ålin 43) (*Gazetteer* no. 16). More tombs were excavated in 1968 and 1969 (*AD* 24, 1969, *Chr.* 1, 111; 25, 1970, *Chr.* 1, 156).

**TIRYNS:** The site at Tiryns has always been visible. It is mentioned by

Pausanias (II 25.7). Although it was not important after the Bronze Age, it was occupied throughout antiquity until destroyed by Argos in 468 B.C.

H. Schliemann and W. Dörpfeld excavated at Tiryns in 1884 and Dörpfeld in 1885, uncovering most of the palace and the fortifications of the main citadel, with their galleries and chambers (H. Schliemann, *Tiryns*, London 1886) (C. Schuchhardt, *Schliemann's Excavations*, London 1891, 93ff). For a description of the state of the citadel after these excavations, see Frazer (Frazer, *Pausanias* 3, 217ff). Some excavations were carried out in the bathroom in 1890 by Kh. Tsountas and D. Philios (*PAE* 1890, 37ff).

Beginning in 1905 the German Institute under L. Curtius, H. Hepding, W. Dörpfeld, A. Frickenhaus, K. Müller, G. Lippold, G. Rodenwalt and E. Schmidt excavated at Tiryns. They uncovered more of the palace itself, examined the lower strata on the citadel, recovered Archaic remains from a sanctuary of Hera, and excavated part of the prehistoric lower town and Geometric graves outside the citadel. Work continued until the outbreak of WW I with some study after. Work was resumed in 1926 by G. Karo, K. Müller and E. Kunze and continued for a few years. More of the lower town was excavated with stratified deposits of EH–LH III periods, and more of the Geometric cemetery. A large Mycenaean chamber tomb cemetery at Ayios Elias a few km southeast of Tiryns was excavated in 1927. Six volumes of the final publications of the German excavations have so far appeared (*Tiryns I*, Athens 1912, to *Tiryns VI*, Mainz 1974).

In 1956 and 1957 N. Verdelis excavated a layer of burnt debris including frescoe fragments and pottery outside the citadel walls (*AD* 20, 1965, *Mel.* 137ff). He also excavated about 30 graves ranging from sub-Mycenaean to Geometric in an area partly previously occupied by Mycenaean houses. One sub-Mycenaean grave contained a shield boss, a spear head, a dagger and a bronze helmet (*AE* 1956, *par.* 5ff) (*AM* 78, 1963, 1ff). Restoration work in 1962 by Verdelis led to the discovery of two underground passages leading to springs (*AD* 18, 1963, *Chr.* 1, 66ff; 19, 1964, *Chr.* 1, 108ff).

In 1965 excavation was resumed as a joint Greek-German enterprise with N. Verdelis, P. Grossmann, G. Neumann and J. Schäfer, but large scale excavation was not undertaken until 1968. The lower enceinte was explored. The wall was constructed in LH IIIB and LH IIIB buildings were uncovered. After a destruction, there are indications of fairly intensive LH IIIC1 occupation in this area (*AR* 1968–69, 13; 1969–70, 14) (cf. Ålin 25ff) (Desborough 79) (Scoufopoulos 46ff).

**TROIZEN:** On Troizen in general, see Frazer (Frazer, *Pausanias* 3, 273ff), A. Frickenhaus and W. Müller (*AM* 36, 1911, 31ff), G. Welter (*Troizen und Kalaureia,* Berlin 1911) and N. Faraklas (*Troizinia, Kalaureia, Methana, Ancient Greek Cities* no. 10, Athens Technological Organization, Athens Center of Ekistics, Athens 1971).

The French School under P. Legrand excavated several buildings in the ancient city beginning in 1890, uncovering remains of the temple of Hippolytos and the Asklepieion by the Episkopi church, and a gymnasium (*BCH* 1892, 165ff; 1893, 84ff; 1897, 543ff; 1900, 179ff; 1905, 269ff; 1906, 52ff). While the topography has been well studied in the works mentioned above, there have been no other organized excavations. One chance find of importance was a copy (or later version) of the decree of the Athenians under Themistokles to evacuate to Troizen in 480 B.C. (cf. *Hesperia* 29, 1960, 198ff).

# *Corinthia*

The following sites, while in the modern name of Corinthia, would usually have been considered part of ancient Achaia: Derveni, Pitsa and Pellene.

The following were considered part of ancient Arcadia: Pheneos and Stymphalos.

**ALCYONIDES ISLANDS (Kala Nisia):** I. Papachristodoulou reported Hellenistic and Roman sherds and remains of buildings at Mandraki on Panagia Island, and ancient buildings and walls on Daskalio Island (*AAA* 1, 1968, 116f).

**ATHIKIA:** At 'Ayios Nikolaos' by Athikia, where the so-called Apollo of Tenea was found (cf. Frazer, *Pausanias* 3, 39ff), LH through Classical sherds have been noted, and ancient remains have been reported at other locations in the vicinity (*AA* 1939, 270ff) (Ålin 58, 61) (*Gazetteer* no. 51).

An early Geometric grave group was found by chance in 1958 (*Hesperia* 33, 1964, 91ff).

**AYIOI THEODOROI:** In 1961 O. Alexandri and N. Verdelis excavated north of the village of Ayioi Theodoroi east of the Isthmus of Corinth, at

'Moulki', finding Geometric and Classical graves, sherds of the 7th to 3rd centuries B.C. and remains of Hellenistic houses. Although no remains later than c. 200 B.C. were found, the excavators identified the site as ancient Crommyon (*AD* 17, 1961–62, *Chr.* 52ff). In the village a number of ruins, now mostly destroyed, were noted by travellers, and the village itself is perhaps the site of the town of Crommyon (*Corinth* I, 46ff) (*AGC* 3, App. II, 12f).

**AYIOS VASILIOS:** In 1921–22 C. Blegen excavated a settlement of EH through LH IIIB date on the Zygouries hill near the village. The MH period was less well represented than the EH and LH periods. Four MH graves, three of them of children, were found within the settlement. In one LH III house, possibly a potter's workshop, over 1300 vases of various types were found stacked up. There was evidence that the LH IIIB settlement was destroyed by fire. At 'Ambelakia' about 500 meters west of the village a cemetery was excavated. Of graves which could be dated, there were three or four EH ossuary-like graves, two MH graves, two LH IIIC chamber tombs and forty Roman tombs. North of the settlement a Geometric grave was excavated (C. Blegen, *Zygouries*, American School of Classical Studies at Athens, Cambridge, Mass. 1928).

At 'Ayia Triada' about 4 km southeast of Ayios Vasilios, A. Frickenhaus in 1912 recovered about 200 figurines from a Mycenaean shrine, mostly phi- and psi-type figurines of LH III date (*AA* 1913, 116) (cf. Ålin 37) (*Gazetteer* no. 49).

**CORINTH (New Corinth):** Mycenaean chamber tombs have been excavated in New Corinth near the railway station, and sub-Mycenaean and proto-Geometric sherds have also been reported (*AR* 1932–33, 276) (*AJA* 58, 1954, 232) (*BCH* 1955, 228) (Ålin 57) (*Gazetteer* no. 66).

**CORINTH (Old Corinth):** W. Dörpfeld, in 1886, was the first to carry out excavations on the site of ancient Corinth, working on the temple later identified as the Temple of Apollo (*AM* 11, 1886, 297ff). A. Skias worked on the site in 1892, in an unsuccessful attempt to locate the ancient agora, and again in 1906, clearing the site after flooding (*PAE* 1892, 111ff; 1906, 145ff).

The American School of Classical Studies began work in 1896, and their excavations have continued with few breaks since. The first series of excavations, from 1896 to 1916, were directed successively by R. B. Richardson, T. W. Heermance, J. L. Caskey, and Bert Hodge Hill. In the interval before resumption of major excavations in 1925, finds were studied and a few trials made. A. L. Walker investigated the prehistoric deposits in the area of the Temple Hill, and C. Blegen explored prehistoric sites in the area of Corinthia. In 1925 work was resumed, directed variously by T. L. Shear (mainly in the theatre, cemeteries and the Roman villa), Bert Hodge Hill (the area of the agora and the precinct of Apollo) and C. Blegen (on Acrocorinth). Directors since then have included Rhys Carpenter, C. H. Morgan, O. Broneer, H. Robinson, and C. K. Williams. Others taking part have included F. J. de Waele, K. Freeman, J. H. Kent, Piet de Jong, R. S. Scranton, Homer Thompson, F. O. Waage, R. Stroud (Sanctuary of Demeter and Kore), S. Weinberg, Mrs. Weinberg, J. K. Anderson, J. R. Wiseman (University of Texas excavation of the Gymnasium), N. Bookidis (Sanctuary of Demeter and Kore), D. Pallas and E. Stikas (early Christian remains).

The site of old Corinth has been occupied since Early Neolithic times. Evidence for a large Neolithic and EH I–II settlement has been found, particularly around the Temple Hill and in the vicinity of the Asklepieion. There is no evidence for an MH settlement within Corinth, and it had long been thought that the site was unoccupied in the Mycenaean period (*AJA* 24, 1920, 1ff; 27, 1923, 151ff, 156ff) but more recently Mycenaean pottery has been found in the central area, particularly behind the Julian basilica (*Hesperia* 6, 1937, 487ff: summary of previous Neolithic and EH finds and results of 1937 trenches on the Temple Hill; 18, 1949, 156f; 20, 1951, 292f: Mycenaean pottery; 29, 1960, 240ff; Neolithic and EH pottery) (Ålin 55) (Desborough 85) (*Gazetteer* no. 56).

On the Cheliotomylos hill, just outside the walls of ancient Corinth, Neolithic and EH strata have been excavated, as have an EH well, MH graves, some LH I, II and IIIB pottery, and a later cemetery (*AJA* 24, 1920, 3; 34, 1930, 409) (*Hesperia* Supplement 8, 1949, 415ff) (*Gazetteer* no. 57) (*AD* 21, 1966, *Chr.* 1, 121ff).

In 146 B.C. Corinth was destroyed by Mummius, and most of the excavated monuments in the city date from the period after its refoundation in 44 B.C. The early campaigns of excavation concentrated on the agora and areas to the north and west. Excavations were also conducted on Acrocorinth. Since the 1930s work has moved to the central and southern areas of the agora. Preliminary reports and various articles have appeared (*AJA* for years 1897, 1898, 1900–1909, 1911, 1915, 1916, 1920, 1921, 1923, and 1925 through 1939) (*Hesperia* for years 1932, 1937–

39, 1941–42, 1944, 1947–49, 1950–57, 1960, 1962, 1964 through 1973) (*AD* 16, 1960 through *AD* 26, 1971, *Chronika* sections) (*AR* 1974–75, 6ff) (Final reports: *Corinth I*, Harvard University Press, 1932, through *Corinth XVI*, 1957 and *XIII*, 1964) (cf. J. L. Caskey, *Ancient Corinth, a Guide to the Excavations*, 6th edition, revised, 1960).

At 'Kritika' in the region of ancient Corinth 68 graves ranging from the 4th century B.C. to the 6th century A.D. were excavated in 1967; traces of occupation in the Geometric period were noted (*AD* 22, 1967, *Chr.* 1, 166ff); in 1970 a large vaulted tomb was excavated (*AD* 26, 1971, *Chr.* 1, 71ff).

**DERVENI:** At 'Psila Alonia' near Derveni, about 1.5 km east of ancient Aigeira (Achaia), N. Verdelis excavated an LH IIIB–C chamber tomb which probably belonged to the settlement at Aigeira. Burials has been made both in the chamber and the dromos (*AE* 1956, *Chr.* 11ff) (*BCH* 1958, 726ff).

**EXAMILIA:** A number of prehistoric sites were noted by Carl Blegen east of ancient Corinth in the area of Examilia (*Corinth* I, 109ff) (*AJA* 24, 1920, 5ff; 27, 1923, 159f) (Ålin 57f) (*Gazetteer* nos. 61, 62, 64). On the Arapiza ridge, west of the New Corinth-Argos road, a small site with EH, MH and LH II–IIIA–B sherds was noted. On the Giriza hill, north of Examilia village, a few trial pits were dug in 1916 indicating a flourishing EH settlement but nothing later. On the Gonia hill, a short distance to the east of Giriza, Blegen carried out trials in 1916 on a large site. Evidence of settlement in Neolithic, EH, MH, LH II–IIIB, possibly continuing into IIIC, and possibly of LH I occupation was found. Seven MH shaft graves were also excavated (*Metropolitan Museum Studies* 3, 1930–31, 55ff).

On the Perdikaria or Kastraki hill between Examilia and Xylokeriza, a section of Cyclopean wall similar to the LH IIIB Isthmus Wall was noted, and EH, MH, and LH III sherds (*Gazetteer* no. 64). An Archaic sarcophagus containing 26 vases was uncovered between Examilia and Chatoupi in 1960 (*Hesperia* 33, 1964, 94ff).

**GALATAKI:** Galataki, near the coast south of Kenchreai, is perhaps the site of ancient Solygeia (*Corinth* I, 97ff). On a hill southwest of the village, N. Verdelis excavated for the Archaeological Society in 1957 five Mycenaean chamber tombs of LH II date, possibly ranging from LH I–IIIA. One of the tomb chambers had been reused as a votive repository. About 50 figurines, mostly of a goddess, and over 1000 vases, all ranging in date from sub-Geometric to early 5th century B.C. were recovered. The following year, the sanctuary, probably of Hera, from which the votives came, was found. It was an apsidal structure of mud brick on stone foundations, first built in the late Geometric period and rebuilt early in the 6th century. Five Geometric tombs have been excavated on a hill further west (*AE* 1956, *par.* 8ff) (*Ergon* 1958, 112ff) (*PAE* 1958, 135ff) (*AD* 16, 1960, *Chr.* 81) (*AGC* 3, App. II, 26-27).

North of Galataki, at 'Stanotopi', are remains of 4th century B.C. fortifications (R. S. Stroud, *Hesperia* 40, 1971, 127ff).

**ISTHMIA:** In 1883 P. Monceaux of the French School investigated the site of the Isthmian Sanctuary of Poseidon. He incorrectly identified the Byzantine fortress at the south end of the trans-isthmus wall, built with material pillaged from the sanctuary, as the sanctuary itself (*Gazette Archéologique*, 1884, 273ff, 354ff; 1885, 205ff). R. J. H. Jenkins and A. H. S. Megaw re-examined the area in 1933, correctly identified the fortress, and dug some trial pits in areas outside the fortress (*BSA* 32, 1932–33, 68ff).

In 1952 the University of Chicago, under the auspices of the American School, began excavations directed by O. Broneer which continued through 1961. They located the site of the sanctuary and excavated the Temenos of Poseidon, with the 5th century temple, traces of an early 7th century temple, the shrine of Palaimon, an early and a later stadium, and the theatre. A commercial complex was excavated nearby at Rachi. Material ranging from EH to sub-Mycenaean has also been found in the area of the sanctuary (Preliminary reports: *Hesperia* 22, 1953, 182ff; 24, 1955, 110ff; 27, 1958, 1ff; 28, 1959, 298ff; 29, 1960, 168ff; 31, 1962, 1ff) (Commercial complex at Rachi: Kh. Kardara, *AJA* 55, 1961, 261ff) (Theatre: E. R. Gebbard, *The Theater at Isthmia*, Chicago, 1973) (Final publications: O. Broneer, *Isthmia* I, American School of Classical Studies at Athens, Princeton, 1971; *Isthmia* II, 1973) (Ålin 59) (*Gazetteer* no. 63).

Excavation was resumed in 1967 by the University of California under Paul A. Clement with O. Broneer. Attention was devoted mostly to the trans-isthmus fortifications (see succeeding article) but work was also carried out in the area of the sanctuary and well over 100 burials mostly of the 6th–5th century were excavated west of Kyras Vrysi village. Excavations continued through 1972 (*AD* 23, 1968, *Chr.* 1, 137ff; 24, 1969, *Chr.* 1, 116ff; 25, 1970, *Chr.* 1, 161ff; 26, 1971, *Chr.* 1, 100f).

**ISTHMUS OF CORINTH:** Several fortification walls have been traced all or part way across the isthmus. The earliest is a Mycenaean wall of Cyclopean construction. Several segments were excavated by the American Isthmia expedition in 1957–58 and 1967. Pottery found in association with the wall is of LH IIIB–C date (O. Broneer, *Hesperia* 35, 1966, 346ff; 37, 1968, 25ff) (*Antiquity* 32, 1958, 80ff) (*Gazetteer* no. 63). Remains of a wall were located west of the Sanctuary of Poseidon in 1957 and were identified as of a wall built in 480 B.C. mentioned by Herodotus (VIII 71). Another segment of this wall was discovered in 1960 and investigated by the Isthmia excavation staff. The course was traced from the harbour of Kenchreai to the area of New Corinth. The wall was found to date probably from the 3rd century B.C., perhaps reusing part of a 5th century wall (J. R. Wiseman, *Hesperia* 32, 1963, 248ff). The Byzantine fortress and trans-isthmus wall were investigated in 1932 and 1933 by R. J. H. Jenkins and A. H. S. Megaw, and identified as the work of Justinian in the 6th century A.D. (*BSA* 32, 1931–32, 68ff). D. Pallas reexamined part of the wall (*AD* 17, 1961–62, *Chr.* 1, 78ff) and a large part of the American Isthmia excavation's attention has been devoted to this wall from 1967–71 (bibliography in previous article). Evidence was found indicating that parts of the wall may be earlier than Justinian.

The 'Diolkos', the way for hauling ships across the isthmus, was investigated by N. Verdelis in 1956–59, and 1960–61. It was probably first constructed in the late 7th or early 6th century B.C. (*AE* 1956, *Chr.* 1ff) (*PAE* 1960, 136ff).

Various remains of the Roman period, probably connected with ancient Schoenos at the south end of the Diolkos, have been noted near the village of Kalamaki, and on a hill north of the village EH, MH, and LH pottery has been noted (*Corinth* I, 49, 114, note 1) (Ålin 60) (*Gazetteer* no 67) (*AGC* 3, App. II, 9-10) (*Hesperia* 27, 1958, 28-29).

**KASTRAKI (Sikyonia):** N. Verdelis partially excavated what is probably a guard tower of the 5th or 4th century B.C. about 5 km from Kastraki (formerly Mazi) on the road to Nemea (*BCH* 1957, 537) (*AR* 1956, 8).

**KATAKALI:** Various remains were noted by K. Gebauer in the vicinity of Katakali and Vlaseika villages, near the coast of the Saronic Gulf. Traces of a small EH settlement and a forge of the Classical period were noted on a small island by the Sideronas Cove. Classical sherds were noted on a hill south of the cove, and Mycenaean sherds were noted on the Malia Toumsa hill further south (*AA* 1939, 271) (Ålin 58) (*Gazetteer* no. 53).

**KATO ALMYRI:** Sherds of Classical and Hellenistic date, probably from graves, have been found in this village east of Galataki on the Saronic Gulf (*AGC* 3, App. II, 27-28). Southeast of the village 6th century tombs have been excavated (*BCH* 1956, 255).

**KENCHREAI:** In 1956 D. Pallas reported two vaulted tombs of the 'columbaria' type and a 2nd or 3rd century A.D. rock cut tomb (*BCH* 1957, 534). In 1962, Roman graves were found when an area was being levelled by bulldozers. A noteworthy find was an Augustan green glazed beaker, or 'modiolus' (*Hesperia* 41, 1972, 355-56).

In 1963, the Universities of Chicago and Indiana began excavations directed by R. S. Scranton and E. Ramage, mainly in the harbour area of ancient Kenchreai. Buildings of the Greek and Roman periods were excavated. A submerged apsidal building was cleared; in it were found crates of 'opus sectile' work (panels of glass set in plaster), some with geometric motifs, others with outdoor scenes or portraits, including Homer, and possibly Plato. Adjoining this building to the south a building tenatively identified as the Temple of Isis was excavated. A large amount of timber was found collapsed into the bottom of the building, masses of tesserae for mosaics, scraps of marble slabs, probably debris from construction or reconstruction. Northeast of the harbour a Roman tomb was excavated. Work continued through 1966 with study and consolidation through 1968 (*Archaeology* 18, 1965, 191ff) (*Hesperia* 33, 1964, 134ff; 36, 1967, 124ff; 40, 1971, 205ff) (*AD* 19, 1964, *Chr.* 1, 103ff; 20, 1965, *Chr.* 1, 145ff; 21, 1966, *Chr.* 1, 141ff; 22, 1967, *Chr.* 1, 185ff; 24, 1969, *Chr.* 1, 119ff).

**KHILIOMODI:** Remains of walls, a theatre, houses, and Geometric and

Roman graves have been reported in the area of Khiliomodi, and ancient Tenea may be closer to this village than to Klenies (q.v.) (*AD* 24, 1969, *Chr.* 1, 103f; 25, 1970, Chr. 1, 159ff) (*AGC* 3, App. II, 25, 32).

**KLENIES:** On a hill nearby, house foundations, sherds, and graves of Archaic and later periods have been found. This site has usually been accepted as the site of Tenea. LH sherds have been reported in the vicinity (Frazer, *Pausanias* 3, 39) (*Corinth* I, 96) (*AA* 1939, 270-71) (*AGC* 3, App. II, 31-32).

Southwest of Klenies on Mt. Nyphitsa a cave of Pan was partially investigated by N. Bertos in 1930. Objects of periods from Neolithic to Roman were found (*BCH* 1930, 479).

**KLEONAI:** The site of ancient Kleonai is about 4 km northwest of Ayios Vasilios. In 1912 A. Frickenhaus with G. Oikonomos excavated a Doric temple, perhaps of Herakles. There are also traces of a fortification wall, and of a temple of Athena (*AA* 1913, 114ff; 1939, 271ff) (cf. Frazer, *Pausanias* 3, 82ff) (cf. Bölte, "Kleonai," *RE* 11, 1921, 721ff). On the highest of the hills comprising the ancient acropolis, MH and LH II–IIIB sherds have been noted (*Gazetteer* no. 47).

**KORAKOU:** In 1915 and 1916 C. Blegen excavated an important, though small, Bronze Age settlement on the Korakou hill, about 2 km west of New Corinth, and about one km east of the site of ancient Lechaion. It was inhabited throughout EH, MH and LH periods. While there is no evidence for any new building in the LH IIIC period, there is no evidence for destruction or abandonment at the end of LH IIIB (*AJA* 24, 1920, 4-5) (C. W. Blegen, *Korakou*, American School of Classical Studies at Athens, 1921) (Ålin 55-56) (Desborough 85-86) (*Gazetteer* no. 60) (cf. *BSA* 67, 1972, 103ff).

**KRINAI (Sikyonia):** About 1.5 km southwest of the village EH, MH, LH and Geometric sherds have been noted (*AD* 22, 1967, *Chr.* 1, 164). In the region of Krinai, about 2 km northeast of Ellenokhori, at 'Krokokkini', a

Mycenaean chamber tomb of LH IIIA–B date was excavated in 1965 (*AD* 21, 1966, *Chr.* 1, 123-24; 22, 1967, *Chr.* 1, 163-64).

**LALIOTI (Sikyonia):** On the Kourkoula hill between Lalioti and Ano Diminio E. Meyer in 1925 noted sherds which he identified as ranging from EH to Classical date. He noted house remains, and part of a possibly Mycenaean wall, all largely destroyed between 1925 and 1937 (Meyer 1939, 10-11) (cf. *AA* 1939, 272) (Ålin 57). LH vases have been reported from Lalioti village (*AA* 1939, 272ff). For other sites noted in the region: (*AGC* 8, App. II, 6ff).

**LECHAION:** Few remains of ancient Lechaion, one of the ports of Corinth, are known, though the site has been identified (*Corinth* I, 95f). In 1916 A. Philadelpheus excavated a Roman building nearby (*AD* 4, 1918, 125ff) which E. Stikas re-examined in 1957. He concluded that it was a 3rd century A.D. Nymphaion (*PAE* 1957, 89ff). D. Pallas excavated early Christian churches and other remains for the Greek Archaeological Society between 1956 and 1961 (*PAE* for years 1956 through 1961, and 1965) (Summary in *AD* 17, 1961–62, *Chr.* 1, 69ff; an account of the harbour, 75ff).

About 2 km west of ancient Lechaion, C. Blegen noted an ancient settlement (*AJA* 24, 1920, 4) which was excavated in 1972 and dated to EH II–III periods (*AD* 26, 1971, *Chr.* 1, 68ff). MH and LH II–IIIB sherds have also been noted (*Gazetteer* no. 59) and S. Kharitonidis excavated a Mycenaean chamber tomb west of Lechaion (*BCH* 1954, 112). Kharitonidis and the American School in 1954 excavated 46 graves, mostly of the 5th and early 4th centuries B.C., between Lechaion and Korakou (*Hesperia* 37, 1968, 345ff).

**LOUTRAKI:** K. Gebauer reported several sites ranging from EH to sub-Mycenaean in the area of Loutraki (*AA* 1939, 269) (*Gazetteer* nos. 68-70) and T. J. Dunbabin located a site on the slopes of Loutraki mountain, noting Mycenaean, proto-Corinthian, Corinthian and Attic sherds (*Perachora* I, vii-viii) (Ålin 60) (*Gazetteer* no. 71).

**MEGALI VALTSA:** The region of Megali Valtsa has been surveyed by A. Skias (*AE* 1919, 45ff) and Ernst Meyer (Meyer, 1939, 1ff). At 'Elliniko' are remains of a watchtower. Remains of a Roman settlement were noted, and ruins of an aqueduct leading toward Sikyon.

**NEMEA:** The site of ancient Nemea is near the village of Heraklion, re-named Archaic Nemea. The Temple of Zeus was long known, and the French School conducted soundings in and around the temple in 1884 and 1912 (*BCH* 1885, 349ff; 1925, 1ff) (Frazer, *Pausanias* 3, 88ff). From 1924 to 1927 the American School under Bert Hodge Hill and C. Blegen excavated the temple and other remains including a palaistra and gymnasium, and located the stadium. On the Tsoungizo hill west of the village, EH, MH and LH II houses were uncovered in trials. On the south slope Neolithic remains were found in and around a collapsed cave. Hill continued his study of the site in preparation for publication; after his death in 1958 C. K. Williams took over the plans and carried out some supplementary excavations (*Art and Archaeology* 1925, 175ff; 1926, 127ff) (*AJA* 31, 1927, 421ff) (*AD* 18, 1963, *Chr.* 1, 81ff; 20, 1965, *Chr.* 1, 154ff) (*Hesperia* 35, 1966, 320ff) (B. H. Hill, *The Temple of Zeus at Nemea,* revised and suppl. by C. K. Williams, American School of Classical Studies at Athens, Princeton 1966). S. G. Miller of the University of California at Berkeley resumed excavation in 1973–74, in the sanctuary area, at the stadium, and on the Tsoungizo hill (*Hesperia* 44, 1975, 143ff) (*AR* 1974–75, 8f).

**PELLENE (Ancient Achaia):** The site of ancient Pellene is on a ridge northeast of Zougra village, renamed Pellene. For early bibliography, see Frazer (Frazer, *Pausanias* 4, 81ff). A. Orlandos excavated here in 1931 and 1932, and uncovered an Archaic temple, perhaps of Athena, and traces of Hellenistic and Roman buildings (*PAE* 1931, 73ff; 1932, 62f). A group of nearly 300 obsidian objects now in the New Carlsberg Glyptothek in Copenhagen is said to have come from Pellene (Åström 107) (C. Blinkenberg, *Archaeologische Studien,* Copenhagen 1904, 14ff) (cf. R. Hope Simpson and J. F. Lazenby, *The Catalogue of the Ships in Homer's Iliad,* Oxford 1970, 69).

**PERACHORA PENINSULA:** Ancient remains on the Perachora peninsula have been visited and described by among others, C. A. Robinson in 1924 in conjunction with the American School Corinth excavations (*Corinth* I, 35ff), the British School during their excavation of the Heraion (*Perachora* I, 4ff), K. Gebauer in 1938–39 (*AA* 1939, 268ff) and more recently, by N. Faraklas (*AGC* 3, App. II, 1ff) (cf. Ålin 60f) (*Gazetteer* nos. 72-76).

Among the more important sites, other than the Heraion are:

1. The Diokastro hill, about 1.7 km east of Skinos village. There are well preserved remains of a fort, probably ancient Oenoe. Archaic and Classical sherds have been noted; the walls are probably of late 5th century date (*Corinth* I, 38-40) (*Perachora* I, 8-9) (*AA* 1939, 270).

2. On the Monasteri hill between Asprokambos and Perachora villages, a settlement of the Archaic and Classical periods has been noted. A number of late 6th–early 5th century burials, many in sarcophagi, were excavated in the area by C. Blakeway and T. J. Dunbabin in 1936 (*AR* 1935–36, 144f) (*Perachora* I, 6-7).

3. A number of sites have been noted in the area of Lake Vouliagmeni:
    a. An early Helladic I–II settlement was noted by T. C. Skeat in 1931 on the western side of the channel connecting the lake to the sea (*Perachora* I, 9). In 1965 J. M. Fossey of the British School in a short excavation found remains of a rampart and a large amount of pottery and obsidian. Work was resumed on the site in 1971 (*BSA* 64, 1969, 53ff) (*AR* 1972–73, 8-9). EH or MH sherds have also been observed southeast of the channel (*AGC* 3, App. II, 6).

    b. By the east shore of the lake by the path from Perachora village, sherds from the Mycenaean to the Archaic and Classical periods were noted. A few trenches were dug by the British School Perachora excavation. Traces of walls and possibly some MH cist graves were noted (*Perachora* I, 9) (*Gazetteer* no. 74). To the south, the remains of two Mycenaean chamber tombs have been noted 100 meters from the shore of the bay (*AGC* 3, App. II, 6).

The Heraion at Perachora was excavated by the British School under Humfry Payne in 1930–33. Two sanctuaries were excavated: the temenos of Hera Limenia with the remains of an 8th century temple, above the harbour, and the 6th century temple of Hera Akraia by the harbour, with the foundations of its Geometric predecessor nearby. Important votive deposits going back to the late 9th century were found, including pottery, bronze and terracottas; fragments of clay models of apsidal buildings were also found, probably dating between 800–750 B.C. (H.

Payne et. al., *The Sanctuaries of Hera Akraia and Limenia, Perachora* I, 1940 and *Perachora* II, 1962 Oxford). Other buildings excavated included an L-shaped stoa of the Hellenistic period, the agora (or court of the lower sanctuary), numerous house remains, and cisterns (summary in *Perachora* I, 9ff). Beneath the Geometric deposit a Neolithic celt, poor EH pottery, and some LH III pottery were found, perhaps indicating a small settlement (*Perachora* I, 9, 20, 51) (*Gazetteer* no. 75). Publication of the excavations was delayed due to Payne's death in 1936. T. J. Dunbabin carried out some supplementary excavation in the town area in 1939, and in 1962 A. H. S. Megaw and J. Coulton began a program of clearance and study in preparation for the publication of the buildings other than the sanctuaries. R. A. Tomlinson continued the work through 1966 and in 1971 (*AD* 19, 1964, *Chr.* 1, 107; 20, 1965, *Chr.* 1, 152f; 21, 1966, *Chr.* 1 145ff; 22, 1967, *Chr.* 1, 190ff) (The stoa: *BSA* 59, 1964, 100ff; *BSA* 62, 1967, 207ff) (The harbour: *BSA* 61, 1966, 192ff) (The west court or agora: *BSA* 62, 1967, 453ff) (Other remains and waterworks: *BSA* 64, 1969, 155ff) (*AR* 1972–73, 8) (cf. J. Salmon, *BSA* 67, 1972, 159ff on history of the Heraion).

**PHENEOS (Ancient Arcadia):** The site of ancient Pheneos, consisting of an acropolis and a lower town, lies near the village of Kalyvia. For travellers' descriptions and early bibliography, see Frazer (Frazer, *Pausanias* 4, 235ff), Bölte ("Pheneos," *RE* 19, 1938, 1963ff) and J. ff. Baker-Penoyre (*JHS* 22, 1902, 228ff). Mrs. E. Protonotariou-Deilaki excavated between 1958 and 1961 and in 1964, clearing part of the acropolis defense wall and a 2nd century B.C. Asklepieion. MH and LH remains were found in deep soundings (*AD* 17, 1961–62, *Chr.* 57ff; 20, 1965, *Chr.* 1, 158ff) (*Gazetteer* no. 83).

**PHLIUS:** In 1890 H. S. and C. M. Washington of the American School conducted trials on the acropolis of ancient Phlius, in the Phliasian plain west of Nemea (*AJA* 27, 1924, 438ff). Again in 1924 the American School under C. Blegen excavated on and around the acropolis. On a hill 500 meters southwest of the acropolis remains of a Neolithic and EH settlement were found below Byzantine remains. A large 5th century B.C. building at the area Palati below the acropolis was partially excavated, and to the north of it the theatre was identified (*Art and Archaeology* 20, 1925, 23ff). In 1964 W. R. Biers of the University of Missouri began to study the finds of the 1924 excavations, some of which have now been published (Prehistoric deposits: *Hesperia* 38, 1969, 443ff) (Votive deposit: *Hesperia* 40, 1971, 397ff). In 1970 the University of Missouri, under the auspices of the American School, directed by W. R. Biers, resumed excavation. Work continued in 1972 and 1973. The Palati and the theatre were excavated (*Hesperia* 40, 1971, 424ff; 42, 1973, 102ff) (*AR* 1973–74, 8-9).

For other sites noted in the Phliasian plain, including a fortress near Koutsi with sherds of Archaic to Roman periods, see A. G. Russell ("The Topography of Phlius and the Phliasian Plain," *Liverpool Annals of Archaeology and Anthropology*, 11, 1924, 37ff), and N. Faraklas, (*Phleiasia, Ancient Greek Cities* 11, Athens Technological Organization, Athens Center of Ekistics, Athens, 1972; in modern Greek).

**PITSA (Sikyonia):** After finds of terracottas had been reported, M. Mitsos in 1934 explored a sacred cave near Pitsa, about 10 km west of Xylokastro in western Sikyonia, and A. Orlandos conducted a systematic excavation. Votive figurines from the 7th–3rd century B.C. were found and one Mycenaean sherd (*AA* 1935, 197-98). Among the finds were painted wooden tablets of the 6th century B.C., one showing a scene of sacrifice (A. Orlandos, "Pitsa," *Enciclopedia dell' arte antica classica e orientale* Vol. IV, Rome 1964).

**SIKYON:** In 303 B.C. Demetrias Poliorketes demolished the old city of Sikyon and built a new city on the plateau between the Asopus and Helisson rivers. The new acropolis was on the higher, southern terrace of the plateau. The village of Vasiliko, renamed Sikyon, lies on the lower, northern part. The older city lay in the plain below, but few traces remain. It is normally assumed that the acropolis of the older city was on the lower terrace, where traces of an Archaic temple have been found (*AD* 10, 1926, 46ff) (Frazer, *Pausanias* 3, 43ff), but Faraklas argues that it was on the Tsagriza hill on the western side of the Helisson (*AGC* 8, 36ff).

The theatre at Sikyon, one of the largest in Greece, was excavated by W. J. McMurtry and M. L. Earle under the auspices of the American School between 1886 and 1891 (*AJA* 3, 1887, 444ff; 5, 1889, 267ff; 7, 1891, 281ff; 8, 1893, 388ff) and by A. Fossum in 1898 (*AJA* 9, 1905, 263ff) (cf. E. Fiechter,. *Das Theater in Sikyon*, Stuttgart 1931). In 1908 A. Arvanitopoulos excavated graves of Classical and later date at Vasiliko and at other places in the plain (*PAE* 1908, 148ff). Between 1920 and 1926 A. Philadelpheus excavated the remains of an Archaic temple on the site of the later agora (*AD* 10, 1926, 46ff). From 1932 to 1939 and again from 1951 to 1954 A. Orlandos excavated in and around ancient Sikyon. Two major buildings excavated by Orlandos are the Bouleuterion and the gymnasium complex. He also excavated graves, house remains, an early Christian basilica, and carried out further work in the theatre and the Archaic temple (*PAE* for years 1932 through 1939, and 1951 through 1954). In 1966 a cemetery dating from the 5th or 4th century B.C. to Roman times was excavated in the plain north of the city and a house with a pebble mosaic floor was also partially excavated in the plain (*AD* 21, 1966, *Chr.* 1, 124; 22, 1967, *Chr.* 1, 164ff).

MH, LH I–IIIA–B sherds have been noted at a site near Vasiliko, and on the Xerokastelli hill are remains of what may be a Mycenaean watch tower (*AA* 1939, 272) (*Gazetteer* no. 77). LH III graves have been reported near the village of Moulki, north of Vasiliko (*JHS* 68, 1948, 60 note 22).

For other sites noted in the area of Sikyon see A. Skias (*AE* 1919, 45ff), C. H. Skalet (*Ancient Sikyon*, Baltimore 1928), K. Gebauer (*AA* 1939, 272ff) E. Meyer (Meyer 1939, 1ff) and N. Faraklas (*Sikyonia, Ancient Greek Cities 8*, Athens Technological Organization, Athens Center of Ekistics, Athens 1972).

**STIMANKA (Sikyonia):** Five hundred meters northwest of the village at 'Ayios Ioannis' a Classical and later building was excavated in 1962. It is a house, or possibly a shrine (*AD* 18, 1963, *Chr.* 1, 74ff). For other remains in the vicinity, see C. H. Skalet (*Ancient Sikyon*, Baltimore 1928, 28).

**STYMPHALOS:** The ruins of the ancient Stymphalos lie south of Kionia village at the edge of the lake. The acropolis is on a long narrow ridge with the remains of the lower town to the northeast and south.

For travellers' descriptions and early bibliography see Frazer (Frazer, *Pausanias* 4, 268ff), Bölte, "Stymphalos," *RE* IV A, 1931, 436ff) and H. Latterman and F. Hiller von Gärtringen (*AM* 40, 1915, 71ff).

Between 1924 and 1929, when work was stopped due to the rise in the level of the lake, A. Orlandos excavated in the lower town for the Greek Archaeological Society, uncovering a Hellenistic temple, parts of the city wall, the agora, and also working on the Frankish church (*PAE* for years 1924–30). In 1958 R. Hope Simpson noted Mycenaean sherds on the acropolis, which has not been excavated (*Gazetteer* no. 84).

**TITANE (Sikyonia):** The site of ancient Titane is probably to be identified with remains on a hill with a chapel of Ayios Tryphon just north of the village of Voivonda (renamed Titane), south of Lopesi (renamed Gonoussa). There are remains of fortification walls on the hill, and ancient architectural fragments are built into the chapel (Frazer, *Pausanias* 3, 69ff) (Meyer, 1939, 11ff). EH and LH IIIB sherds have been noted (*Gazetteer* no. 80).

**ZEVGOLATIO:** By the ruined Ayios Charalambos chapel near Zevgolatio near Assos, west of New Corinth, S. Kharitonidis excavated a Roman bath complex in 1954 (*BCH* 1955, 102ff), and at 'Zarazani' to the west made some excavations in a 6th–5th century B.C. cemetery (*BCH* 1955, 231).

# Elis

The following sites in the modern nome of Elis were usually considered part of Arcadia in antiquity: Alipheira, Bassae, Perivolia, Phigaleia.

**AGRAPIDOKHORI:** On the Armatova hill, northeast of the village near the confluence of the Ladon and Peneios rivers, N. Yialouris in 1962 and P. Themelis in 1964 carried out trial excavations. They found material on the hill ranging at least from the Geometric period to the 3rd century B.C. A Classical house was excavated on the hill. In the valley between Armatova and the village, Roman tombs were excavated (*AD* 18, 1963, *Chr.* 1, 104; 20, 1965, *Chr.* 2, 214ff).

Mrs. V. Leon-Mitsopoulou, R. Zwanziger and S. Karwies of the Austrian Institute examined the site for the Peneios Dam survey project in 1967 (*AD* 23, 1968, *Chr.* 1, 177ff).

J. Coleman of the University of Colorado, under the auspices of the American School, worked on the site in 1968. Several graves were excavated on the hill; only one produced any finds, including some Minyan ware. Fifth and fourth century B.C. buildings were uncovered, and a Byzantine house. Northeast of the hill Roman graves and a well containing Archaic pottery were excavated. The Armatova hill is perhaps the site of Elean Pylos (AAA 1, 1968, 285ff) (*AD* 24, 1969, *Chr.* 1, 155ff).

L. Parlama has reported a circular Mycenaean chamber tomb found in 1971. LH IIIA–B pottery was found associated with inhumations and LH IIIC pottery with remains of cremations (*AE* 1971, *par.* 52ff).

**ALIPHEIRA:** The site of ancient Alipheira is above modern Alipheira (formerly Rangozio) northwest of Andritsaina. For early descriptions and bibliography, see Frazer (Frazer, *Pausanias* 4, 297ff). A. Orlandos worked at the site from 1932 to 1935, excavating the fortifications, a mid–5th century temple of Athena, a Hellenistic temple of Asclepios, and a cemetery (*AA* 1933, 232ff; 1934, 156ff; 1935, 199; 1936, 136) (A. K. Orlandos, *I Arkadiki Alipheira kai ta Mnimeia tis,* Library of the Athenian Archaeological Society no. 58, 1967–68).

**ALPHEIOUSSA:** At 'Samakia', southwest of Volantza renamed Alpheioussa, N. Yialouris has reported a 5th century B.C. tomb (*BCH* 1959, 658) (*AR* 1959, 11) and ruins of buildings (*AR* 1960, 14).

**AMALIAS:** Between 1962 and 1964 A. Leroi-Gourham, M. Brézillon, N. and J. Chavaillon and F. and R. P. Hours of the French School found Paleolithic remains in the region south of Amalias (*BCH* 1964, 1ff; 1967, 151ff).

**ASPRA SPITIA:** Remains of EH, LH, Classical and Hellenistic occupation have been noted on the Tourla hill near the junction of the Erymanthos and Alpheios rivers (Sperling no. 38) (*AJA* 1961, no. 10).

**BASSAE:** The site of the Temple of Apollo Epikourios at Bassae, built by the Phigaleians in the late 5th century, was discovered in 1765 by J. Rocher, a French architect. A German and English expedition including Baron Haller von Hallerstein and C. R. Cockerell discovered the frieze in 1812, and cleared the ruins in 1813. The following year the frieze was sold at auction to the British Museum (von Stackelberg, *Der Apollotempel zu Bassae in Arcadia und die daselbst ausgegrabenen Bildwerke,* Frankfurt am Main 1826). For other early bibliography and description, see Frazer (Frazer, *Pausanias* 4, 393ff) and for a summary of published reports and the fate of early sketches and notes, see W. Dinsmoor (*Metropolitan Museum Studies* 4, 1932–33, 204ff).

Between 1902 and 1908 the temple was restored and further, more

scientific, excavation carried out. Those taking part included P. Kavvadias, K. Romaios and K. Kourouniotis. Additional fragments of sculpture were discovered and it was demonstrated that an earlier 7th century
temple had existed on the site. Finds from this included pottery, statuettes and armour (*PAE* 1902, 23ff) (*AE* 1910, 291ff; 1914, 57ff; 1933, 1ff).
Above the temple of Apollo, on Kotilion, two other sanctuaries were
excavated by Kourouniotis. One is the temple of Aphrodite mentioned by
Pausanias (VIII 41.10) (*AE* 1903, 151ff).

In 1957–59 and 1967 N. Yialouris explored the area of the temple for
further fragments of sculpture and for information about the earlier temple, and he studied the sculptures and notebooks in the British
Museum. Traces of Archaic and Classical buildings were uncovered to
the west of the temple. Fragments of Archaic vases, iron weapons, and a
7th century iron statuette of a man were found, as well as fragments of
the frieze of the Classical temple, casts of some of which have been in-
corporated in the British Museum frieze (*PAE* 1959, 155ff) (*Ergon* 1959,
106ff) (*AE* 1967, 187ff) (*BCH* 1959, 623ff).

N. Yialouris and L. Parlama excavated at Bassae in 1970, examining
the condition of the temple foundation, and investigating the surrounding area. In the area south of the temple they discovered the foundations
of a temple-like building. The finds, including weapons, miniature
vases, clay antefixes and fragments of two Archaic clay acroteria, make it
likely that this was the pre-Classical temple (*AAA* 6, 1973, 39ff) (*AR*
1973–74, 14) (*AD* 26, 1971, *Chr.* 1, 142ff).

F. A. Cooper of the University of Minnesota studied the temple, re-
cording all fallen blocks and fragments. He also surveyed the vicinity of
Bassae (*AR* 1972–73, 18; 1973–74, 14) (*AAA* 5, 1972, 359ff).

**DIASELA:** Northwest of Diasela (formerly Broumazi), on the Koutso-
chira hill, about 2 km south of the Alpheios, N. Yialouris in 1956 dug
three collapsed chamber tombs. The smallest of the three had apparently not been plundered, and a number of whole vases were recovered.
The contents of the tombs were mainly LH IIIB, but one tomb contained
some probably LH IIIC pottery. Nearby Yialouris discovered a Mycenaean settlement with a heavy fortification wall, and he explored a Mycenaean house. Sherds from the site range from LH IIIB to perhaps sub-
Mycenaean. There are traces of two possible tholoi. A Classical tomb
was also discovered (*PAE* 1955, 243) (*BCH* 1956, 289; 1957, 574ff; 1959,
649ff) (*AJA* 1961, no. 17) (Desborough, 92).

**ELIS:** Excavation in the ancient city of Elis, founded in the 5th century, (by Palaiopolis, now named Elis) was carried out by the Austrian Institute between 1910 and 1914. Hellenistic and Roman buildings were excavated, and the theatre and gymnasium located (*JÖAI* 14, 1911, Beiblatt 97ff; 16, 1913, Beiblatt 145ff; 18, 1915, Beiblatt 61ff). Excavations were resumed as an Austrian-Greek project in 1960 under N. Yialouris and V. Leon (later Mrs. Leon-Mitsopoulou). Work was concentrated on the theatre area. Roman graves were found in the vicinity, also an EH cist grave, and a group of sub-Mycenaean–proto-Geometric graves. The area of the South Stoa of the agora was further explored. Work continued through 1973 (*JÖAI* 45, 1960, Beiblatt 99ff; 46, 1961–63, Beiblatt 33ff, 57ff; 47, 1964–65, Beiblatt 43ff, 73ff, 91ff; 48, 1966–67, Beiblatt 45ff, 63ff; 49, 1968–71, Beiblatt 93ff) (*PAE* for years 1962 through 1966, 1969, 1970, 1973) (*Ergon* for years 1960, 1962 through 1966, 1969, 1970, 1972, 1973) (*AD* 16, 1960, *Chr.* 134-35; 17, 1961–62, *Chr.* 124ff; 18, 1963, *Chr.* 1, 101ff; 19, 1964, *Chr.* 2, 180ff; 20, 1965, *Chr.* 2, 211ff).

Emergency excavations on account of the planned Peneios River dam project were conducted on a wide scale in the city from 1964 through 1971 by G. Papathanasopoulos and Th. Karageorga (*AD* 23, 1968, *Chr.* 1, 162ff; 24, 1969, *Chr.* 1, 152ff; 26, 1971, *Chr.* 1, 138ff) (*AAA* 1, 1968, 128ff, including summary of previous excavation; 2, 1969, 15ff; 4, 1971, 27ff).

**EPITALION:** About one-half km north of Epitalion (formerly Agoulinitsa), northwest of the railway line are a group of hills called the Agiorgitika. W. Dörpfeld apparently noted unspecified ancient remains here (*AM* 38, 1913, map plate IV) and E. Meyer noted indications of ruined tombs on the furthest southeast of the hills (Meyer 1957, 49, 50, 60). LH IIIA–B sherds were found (*AJA* 1961, no. 12). Northeast of the village, at 'Dardiza', Archaic, Classical and Hellenistic sherds were noted over a wide area, possibly connected with Classical Epitalion (*AJA* 1961, no. 13). In 1966–67, P. Themelis excavated in the vicinity. West of the new National Road he discovered remains of Roman date including baths and houses. On Barbeika, one of the Agiorgitika, he excavated a Mycenaean house. Roman graves were also excavated in the vicinity, and MH and LH sherds were found in the cover above the tombs, near where an LH deposit had been found in 1965 (*AD* 22, 1967, *Chr.* 1, 210f; 23, 1968, *Chr.* 1, 165ff) (*AAA* 1, 1968, 201ff).

**GOUMERO:** N. Yialouris reported a 4th century B.C. tomb at 'Panagia' or

'Ammouli' near Goumero, about 14 km north of Olympia. An LH IIIC vase was found in the same vicinity (*BCH* 1959, 658) (*AR* 1959, 11).

**GRILLOS:** South of Grillos (formerly Moundriza) are ruins of walls and buildings, perhaps ancient Hypana (Meyer 1957, 43-44). North of Grillos at Ayios Ilias are foundations of a Classical building, perhaps a temple, and remains of the Archaic to Hellenistic periods have been found nearby at Xilokastro (*PAE* 1955, 243) (*BCH* 1956, 290; 1958, 568; 1959, 658).

**LAKE KAIAPHA:** Ruins have been noted in the lagoon near the modern health spa. They are probably Classical or Hellenistic and may be either buildings or a roadway (Dörpfeld, *AM* 33, 1908, 320ff) (Sperling no. 7) (Meyer 1957, 78) (Bisbee, *Hesperia* 6, 1937, 525).

**KAKOVATOS:** The German Institute under W. Dörpfeld excavated in 1907 and 1908 on an acropolis called Ktiria (now Nestora) about 1.5 km northeast of Kakovatos village. Three Mycenaean tholos tombs (LH I–II) were excavated and remains of a settlement on the hill were explored. Pottery from the site included MH and LH, and some LH IIIB pottery apparently comes from a lower town. Dörpfeld identified this site as Nestor's Pylos. The settlement remains were not adequately published (*AM* 32, 1907, vi-xvi; 33, 1908, 295ff; 34, 1909, 269ff; 38, 1913, 101ff). In light of more recent discoveries in Messenia, this site must be considered one of many local Mycenaean centers (*AJA* 46, 1942, 538ff, for discussion; *AJA* 1961, no. 20).

**KASTRO:** The Medieval castle of Chelmoutsi, near Kastro, was visited by J. Servais in 1960 in conjunction with his study of the location of ancient Kyllini (q.v.). He mentioned MH and possibly Mycenaean sherds from beneath the castle walls, and pottery from a Mycenaean tomb from between Kastro and Neokhori (*BCH* 1961, 123ff). He returned to the site and conducted trials in 1962, in which further MH and LH material was found, but only rare traces of Archaic and Classical material (*BCH* 1964, 9ff) (*Gazetteer* no. 280). A cemetery of Geometric graves has been reported from the vicinity of Chelmoutsi (*AR* 1956, 16) (*BCH* 1957, 568). During his studies in 1960, Servais found Paleolithic implements on the plateau east of Kastro (*BCH* 1961, 1ff). A. Leroi-Gourham with J. and N. Chavaillon and F. and R. P. Hours further studied the Paleolithic remains in this area in 1962–64 (*BCH* 1964, 1ff; 1969, 97ff).

**KATAKOLO:** N. Yialouris in 1957 explored the area of Ayios Andreas village one km northwest of Katakolo. On the hill with the medieval fort above the village prehistoric pottery was found—Neolithic, EH, MH, LH I–IIIb, sub-Mycenaean, and proto-Geometric—and remains of up to the Hellenistic period. In the waters of the bay remains of buildings from Archaic to Roman times were explored, and others were found along the shore. The site, including the acropolis, seems to have been continuously occupied from Neolithic to Medieval times, though the Classical settlement, probably ancient Pheia, seems concentrated around the harbour (*AE* 1957, 31ff) (*BCH* 1959, 649ff). J. Hall and G. Papathanasopoulos noted further remains in 1967 (*AD* 23, 1968, *Chr.* 1, 162) (Desborough 90-91).

A. Leroi-Gourham reported Paleolithic finds from Katakolo (*BCH* 1964, 1ff).

**KAUKANIA:** A large Hellenistic cemetery was discovered near this village north of Olympia in 1959 (*AR* 1959, 11) (*BCH* 1959, 656). For other remains in the vicinity see Kladeos.

**KLADEOS:** On the Phengaraki hill between Kladeos (formerly Stravo-kephalo) and Kaukaunia, N. Yialouris noted six slab-covered cist graves, probably Mycenaean. Plentiful Hellenistic and Roman sherds were noted below the hill (*BCH* 1961, 722) (*AD* 16, 1960, *Chr.* 126). Other Mycenaean chamber tomb cemeteries have been reported in the vicinity at 'Trypes', 2 km north of Kladeos (LH IIIA–C); another near Kladeos (LH IIIA–B), partly destroyed by road building (*BCH* 1963, 795) (*AD* 18, 1963, *Chr.* 1, 103; 19, 1964, *Chr.* 2, 177f) (*UMME* nos. 325-27).

**KOSKINA:** G. Papathanasopoulos reported the remains of four Mycenaean chamber tombs at Lakkopholia northeast of Koskina. One was excavated (*AD* 25, 1970, *Chr.* 1, 193).

**KOUMOUTHEKRA:** K. Müller and F. Weege of the German Institute excavated the Temple of Artemis Limnatis between Koumouthekra (or Kombothekra) and Graika in the Lapithos mountains. It is a 5th century Doric edifice. Fifth and fourth century small bronzes and terracottas were recovered (*AM* 33, 1908, 323ff). E. Meyer noted other remains including sanctuaries in the Lapithos mountains in 1954 (Meyer 1957, 50ff).

**KYLLINI:** In 1960 J. Servais studied the promontory of western Elis to determine the location of ancient Kyllini, the naval base of the Eleans. By modern Kyllini village are the ruins of the medieval town and fortress of Glarentza. He listed the scattered ancient remains, mostly 5th century and later, with a few possibly LH III sherds, discussed alternative locations of Kyllini and concluded that Glarentza is the most likely location (*BCH* 1961, 123ff). For other remains on the promontory see Kastro.

**LADIKO:** At Ladiko, west of Makrisia, N. Yialouris reported three graves in which Hellenistic sherds were found in 1961 (*AD* 17, 1961–62, *Chr.* 107).

**LEPREON:** For the remains of ancient Lepreon, above Strovitsi, renamed Lepreon, see Frazer (Frazer, *Pausanias* 3, 473ff). The visible remains are mostly Classical and Hellenistic, though the city was inhabited from Archaic to Roman times. At the east end of the modern village, traces of EH, LH and Classical occupation have been noted, the EH being particularly abundant (Sperling no. 37) (*AJA* 1961, no. 21).

**MAGEIRA:** P. Themelis reported six perhaps late Mycenaean burial pithoi at 'Kioupia', where a Minoan type figurine had previously been found. Traces of fire and burnt bone were found in the pithoi (*AD* 21, 1966, *Chr.* 1, 170) (*AAA* 2, 1969, 254). At 'Kouveli' or 'Bambakia' about 200 m south of the village, road works revealed Hellenistic built graves in 1966. Burial pithoi, probably Roman, were found on the hill above. P. Themelis reported the finds (*AD* 22, 1967, *Chr.* 1, 211ff). A Hellenistic cist grave has also been reported and a probably MH tumulus is also known (*AD* 24, 1969, *Chr.* 1, 149) (*AJA* 1969, no. 7B).

**MAKRISIA:** Ancient Skillous is most probably to be located in the valley between Makrisia and the Alpheios, although finds have so far been few. For a discussion of the topography, see E. Meyer (Meyer 1957, 47f, 63ff) and P. Themelis (*AD* 23, 1968, *Mel.* 284ff, 315f). Meyer examined the Profitis Elias hill about 500 m west of the village and noted sparse finds of sherds from Classical to Roman times, and late Mycenaean and sub-Mycenaean sherds from graves on the west slope. W. McDonald and R. Hope Simpson noted some possibly MH ware, but nothing definitely post-Bronze Age (*AJA* 1961, no. 14).

In 1968 a tumulus was discovered on the hill by villagers. One partially undisturbed cist grave was excavated; the rest had been destroyed. About 20 whole vases, not later than transitional LH I/II, had been turned over to the authorities. There were some LM IA imports (*AD* 23, 1968, *Mel.* 284ff) (*AAA* 1, 1968, 126f).

To the north of the Profitis Elias hill, on the Kania spur west of the Selountia River, N. Yialouris reported in 1954 a previous excavation of two Mycenaean chamber tombs, and at least two more were noted (*BCH* 1954, 128) (*PAE* 1954, 295ff) (cf. Desborough 92). Yialouris also excavated at the same time a votive deposit at 'Kambouli' containing hundreds of miniature vases, other vases, and female terracotta figurines. Finds ranged from the 6th–4th century (*PAE* 1954, 292ff) (cf. Meyer 1957, 48). P. Themelis suggests that the shrine from which these votives came was the predecessor of Xenophon's Artemision (*AD* 23, 1968, *Mel.* 288ff, 315f).

At Bambes, between Makrisia and Skillountia (Mazi), but in the territory of Makrisia, a temple had been reported west of Bambes hamlet on the height south of the Alpheios opposite Olympia (*AM* 38, 1913, map plate IV) (*AR* 1945–47, 115). It was excavated by N. Yialouris in 1953–54. It is a small Doric temple of Zeus dating from the early 5th century. Just to the east of the temple fragments of a large Neolithic vase were found. Another temple was excavated on the Ayios Elias hill directly opposite Olympia (not to be confused with the Profitis Elias hill above, sometimes also called Ayios Elias), and traces of a city were noted on the northeast slopes below it (*BCH* 1954, 130; 1955, 252f) (*PAE* 1954, 290f). In succeeding years Yialouris continued to excavate in the town. Finds range from Geometric to late Classical, and include remains of Archaic and Classical houses, fragments of Archaic statues and part of a large late 7th century clay vessel with relief decoration. An LH tomb was also found (*PAE* 1955, 243f; 1956, 187ff; 1958, 194ff) (*Ergon* 1954, 40f; 1955, 86ff; 1956, 83ff; 1958, 154ff) (Meyer 1957, 46f) (*BCH* 1956, 287; 1957, 570ff; 1959, 656ff).

A probably Hellenistic tomb has been found by Bambes (*AD* 22, 1967, *Chr.* 1, 211) and finds of Classical date between Makrisia and the Alpheios (*AD* 25, 1970, *Chr.* 1, 191ff) (For list of finds in area: *AJA* 1961, nos. 14-16) (*UMME* nos. 311-14, 719-20).

For other remains nearby, see Skillountia.

**MANOLADA:** A. Khoremis has reported the excavation of a Roman bath complex at Manolada in northern Elis in 1968 (*AD* 24, 1969, *Chr.* 1, 149f).

**MARINAKI:** N. Yialouris has reported 6th and 5th century B.C. vases from tombs near Marinaki (*AD* 17, 1961–62, *Chr.* 1, 107).

**MIRAKA:** Various ancient remains have been reported from the vicinity of Miraka village, east of Olympia. In 1908 W. Dörpfeld excavated on the Oinomaos hill and found MH pottery including matt-painted and incised ware, as well as traces of Classical occupation. Dörpfeld identified this as prehistoric Pisa (*AM* 33, 1908, 318ff). East of this, at 'Frangonisi', is an extensive Roman cemetery apparently first noted by I. Kondis during World War II (*AR* 1945–47, 115). N. Yialouris excavated in 1957 and P. Themelis in 1966–67. Beneath the graves were found traces of buildings with fragments of Archaic and Classical pottery, perhaps ancient Pisa, which was destroyed by the Eleans (*BCH* 1959, 656) (*AR* 1959, 11) (*AD* 21, 1966, *Chr.* 1, 177; 22, 1967, *Chr.* 1, 212; 23, 1968, *Chr.* 1, 164; 24, 1969, *Chr.* 1, 147) (*AJA* 1961, no. 9).

A Hellenistic cemetery was discovered by Yialouris between Miraka and the Alpheios in 1954 (*BCH* 1954, 128), and other antiquities have been reported (*AD* 21, 1966, *Chr.* 1, 171) (*UMME* nos. 323-24, 723).

**NEDA RIVER:** In a survey of the region of Phigaleia and Bassae F. A. Cooper of the University of Minnesota discovered remains of ramps for ships and ship sheds west of the Neda gorge, bearing out Pausanias' statement (VIII 41.3) that the Neda was navigable near the sea (*AAA* 5, 1972, 359ff).

**OLYMPIA:** Richard Chandler was the first to identify the site of the Sanctuary of Zeus at Olympia, in 1766. A French expedition under A. Blouet carried out the first excavation in 1829, partly excavating the Temple of Zeus and recovering some fragments of the metopes (A. Blouet et al., *Expédition scientifique de Morée* Vol. I, Paris 1831, 56ff).

Proposals for further excavation were put forward by various people, including Johann Winckelmann, and Ernst Curtius interested the Prussian Royal family, particularly the later Kaiser Wilhelm I, in the project. Finally in 1874 agreement was reached with the Greek government and excavations were begun the following year. The first series of excavation lasted from 1875 to 1881. Besides Curtius and Friedrich Adler who remained in Berlin, those involved included G. Hirschfeld, A. Boetticher, R. Weil, G. Treu, R. Bohn, W. Dörpfeld, R. Borrmann and A. Furtwängler. Most of the buildings in the sanctuary were uncovered and identified by this expedition. A museum was built on the site and opened in 1887 (E. Curtius and F. Adler, *Olympia, die Ergebnisse der vom deutschen Reich veranstalteten Ausgrabungen,* 5 vols. and maps, plates, Berlin 1890–97) (cf. E. N. Gardiner, *Olympia, Its History and Remains,* 1925).

W. Dörpfeld resumed excavation in 1906, and continued after W.W. I in 1921–23, and 1927–29. He concentrated on investigating the earliest history of the site, and he explored particularly the area of the Temple of Hera and the Pelopion. Dörpfeld believed that the early bronzes found at Olympia were prehistoric rather than Geometric, and that the temple of Hera was much older than is now believed. However, he discovered evidence of a prehistoric settlement, MH apsidal houses, coarse MH ware and Minyan ware. The settlement was probably destroyed by flood. Nothing Mycenaean was found (W. Dörpfeld, *Alt-Olympia,* 2 vols., Berlin 1935) (*AM* 31, 1906, 205ff; 33, 1908, 185ff).

In 1936 major excavation was resumed by the German Institute under A. von Gerkan in 1936, and R. Hampe, U. Jantzen and E. Kunze in 1937. Kunze continued to direct the excavation with E. Schleif until 1942, and after the war beginning in 1952, with financial assistance from Carl Diem. A. Mallwitz has assisted since 1956. These major excavations were concluded in 1966, though supplementary work, restoration, study and publication has continued. One of the main areas of work during these years was the stadium. The Archaic and Classical prede- cessors of the 4th century B.C. stadium were excavated and the stadium was then reconstructed in its 4th century form. North of the Leonidaion, the site of the workshop of Pheidias was identified. Tools, scraps of ivory, molds for making metal plate, and an Attic black cup with the name Pheidias on it were recovered. Many of the bronzes found at Olympia recently have come from the large number of wells on the site. Final publications: (*Berichte über die Ausgrabungen in Olympia*, Berlin 1937: 8 vols. to date) (*Olympische Forschungen*, E. Kunze and H. Schleif, ed., Berlin 1944: 7 vols. to date). Recent excavations have been summarized, in addition to annual reports in *BCH* and *AR*: (*AD* 16, 1960, *Chr.* 127ff for the 1952–58 excavations; 17, 1961–62, *Chr.* 107ff for the 1958–61 excava- tions; 18, 1963, *Chr.* 1, 107 ff for the 1962–63 excavations; 19, 1964, *Chr.* 2, 165ff for the 1963–64 excavation). Of the immense literature on Olympia, the following summarize the history of the excavation and give fuller bibliography:

> H.-V. Hermann, *Olympia*, Munich 1972.
> Alfred Mallwitz, *Olympia*, Munich 1972.
> *100 Jahre deutsche Ausgrabung in Olympia*, Ausstellung veranstaltet
>    vom Organisationskomitee für die Spiele der xx. Olympiade,
>    Munich 1972.

More evidence of prehistoric occupation has recently come to light, both in the excavation of the sanctuary area, and in excavations in prep- aration for the construction of the new museum north of the sanctuary, and in other excavations in the vicinity of Olympia. In addition to the MH settlement discovered by Dörpfeld, prehistoric sherds including EH and Mycenaean were found in the stadium excavations. However, the main Mycenaean concentration seems to have been on the neighboring hills. On the site of the new museum, in addition to Archaic bronzes, apparently a votive deposit from the sanctuary, and a late Roman cremation cemetery, N. Yialouris discovered EH, MH pottery including Minyan ware, MH buildings and Mycenaean sherds. Nearby Yialouris excavated two Mycenaean chamber tombs and noted others. He also noted ruins of Mycenaean and pre-Mycenaean buildings on the summit of the Kronos hill. Yialouris also identified a Mycenaean settlement on the Drouva hill by the S.P.A.P. hotel on the western side of the Kladeos. Masses of LH IIIB pottery were recovered. MH and LH finds have been reported from the area of the Olympia railway station. For prehistoric finds in general, see Dörpfeld (*Alt-Olympia* I, 73ff) and H.-V. Herrmann

(*AM* 77, 1962, 3ff) (cf. Desborough 91) (*AJA* 1961, nos. 7-8). Desborough points out that although Mycenaean occupation is now well attested at Olympia, LH IIIC and proto-Geometric finds are very sparse and there may well have been a break during these periods. For the Greek excavations in the area of the new museum, at Drouva, and other places at Olympia: (*BCH* 1959, 655; 1960, 720; 1961, 722; 1962, 743; 1966, 824; 1968, 824) (*AD* 16, 1960, *Chr.* 125f; 17, 1961–62, *Chr.* 105f; 18, 1963, *Chr.* 1, 102ff; 19, 1964, *Chr.* 2, 174ff; 20, 1965, *Chr.* 2, 209ff; 21, 1966, *Chr.* 1, 170; 24, 1969, *Chr.* 1, 146ff; 25, 1970 *Chr.* 1, 191, 194).

For other sites in the Olympia area, see Kaukania, Kladeos, Mageira, Miraka, Platanos, and Phloka.

**PENEIOS RIVER DAM SURVEY:** A survey of the area to be inundated by the Peneios Dam has been carried out. Some finds in this area were reported by P. Themelis (*AD* 20, 1965, *Chr.* 2, 215ff) but the main survey work was carried out in 1967 by the foreign schools in Greece at the request of the Greek Archaeological Service. Those taking part included: Mrs. V. Leon-Mitsopoulou (Austrian Institute), P. Ducrey and F. Vandenabeele (French School), L. Beschi (Italian School), F. Hamdorf (German Institute), J. R. Wiseman (American School), and R. Howell (British School). Sites were from all periods of antiquity. Trial trenches were dug on some sites, and excavators returned to the more important (*AR* 1967–68, 11-12; 1969–70, 15) (*AAA* 1, 1968, 46ff) (*AD* 23, 1968, *Chr.* 1, 174ff).

The British School worked at 'Kostoureika' north of Avgi (formerly Kato Loukavitsa) east of the Loukia stream again in 1969. J. E. Jones, R. A. Tomlinson, P. A. Rahtz, and R. Howell took part. The site consists of a Hellenistic farmhouse above an EH II deposit. Between the village Keramidia and Kalatha, west of the Loukia stream, a large spread of tiles and sherds was investigated at 'Diaselo', 'Keramidia', and 'Kioupia'. The excavators returned to 'Keramidia' and uncovered several buildings of a Roman settlement (*AR* 1968–69, 16; 1969–70, 14-15). For excavations on the Armatova hill near Agrapidokhori, see Agrapidokhori.

**PERIVOLIA:** During a survey of the vicinity of Bassae and Perivolia in 1972, F. A. Cooper of the University of Minnesota noted the remains of a Doric temple, probably of the 4th or 3rd century by the road from Perivolia to Bassae (*AAA* 5, 1972, 359ff).

**PHIGALEIA:** Ancient Phigaleia, at Pavlitsa, renamed Phigaleia, has been little investigated. For a description and bibliography, see Frazer (Frazer, *Pausanias* 4, 390ff). A. Orlandos excavated the ancient spring in Phigaleia in 1927 (*AD* 11, 1927–28, 1ff) (*BCH* 1930, 483).

**PHLOKA:** Near the dam on the Alpheios, about 2 km southwest of the village, west of Olympia, LH IIIB vases and a terracotta figurine from a destroyed tomb have been reported (*AD* 18, 1963, *Chr.* 1, 103). At 'Panoukla' 4th or 3rd century B.C. graves were found (*AD* 23, 1968, *Chr.* 1, 171).

**PLATANOS:** Hellenistic and Roman tombs were reported from 'Kamari' near Platanos, northwest of Olympia (*AD* 16, 1960, *Chr.* 126). In 1963 N. Yialouris investigated three Mycenaean chamber tombs on the southeast edge of the village, finding LH IIIB–C vases (*AD* 19, 1964, *Chr.* 2, 177). Three Minoan type figurines are reported from Platanos (*AAA* 2, 1969, 248ff).

**PLATIANA:** A Classical and Hellenistic fortified town, perhaps going back to Archaic times, was noted by J. Sperling south of Platiana (Sperling no. 30). E. Meyer surveyed the site in 1954. There are remains of fortification walls, the agora, a theatre, and houses. It may either be ancient Epion or Tympaneai (Meyer 1957, 22ff). Further ancient remains were found in 1960 at 'Pteri' (*AD* 16, 1960, *Chr.* 126).

**PRASIDAKI:** N. Yialouris discovered a Classical temple near Prasidaki, south of Lepreon. There were some Archaic traces (*AAA* 4, 1971, 245ff).

**SALMONE:** On the Palaiopyrgo or Gridou hill, about one km southwest of Salmone, formerly Koukoura, W. Dörpfeld noted a Classical temple and a prehistoric settlement (*AM* 38, 1913, 115). These have not been noted since, though Classical and Hellenistic sherds and tiles have been found, an MH pithos noted, and in 1960 a sub-Mycenaean or proto-Geometric pithos burial was found northwest of the site at 'Bambakia' (Sperling no. 12) (*AJA* 1961, no. 5) (*AD* 16, 1960, *Chr.* 126) (Desborough 92). N. Yialouris has reported Roman graves found at 'Ayios Elias' in 1962, and remains of Archaic buildings (*AD* 18, 1963, *Chr.* 1, 104). P. Themelis reported a Hellenistic building found in the area in 1967 (*AD* 23, 1968, *Chr.* 1, 171).

**SAMIKON:** The site of ancient Samikon or Samia is probably on the westernmost spur of the Smerna ridge by modern Samikon. Between it and the shore is the small hill Kleidi. W. Dörpfeld did some exploratory digging both at Samikon and Kleidi in 1908 (*AM* 33, 1908, 320ff; 38, 1913, 111ff) and H. L. Bisbee has published a study of the fortifications of Samikon (*Hesperia* 6, 1937, 525ff). The well-preserved fortifications date probably to the 5th or 4th century, though the settlement probably goes back to the Archaic period (cf. R. L. Scranton, *Greek Walls*, 1941, 62ff) (F. E. Winter, *Greek Fortifications*, 1971, 237-8). Winter suggests that the site was a border fort for Makistos. Other remains were noted on the slopes and in the lagoon below (cf. Meyer 1957, 34ff; 74ff).

Kleidi is perhaps the Homeric Arene. Dörpfeld noted Cyclopean fortifications which have since disappeared. The pottery dates from EH, MH, LH I–II, and LH IIIA–B. A Mycenaean burial mound to the north of this settlement, partly destroyed by villagers, was examined by N. Yialouris in 1954. About fifteen graves were found in three levels. Earliest are transitional MH/LH I, and they continue to LH IIIB (*AD* 20, 1965, *Mel.* 6ff) (*AR* 1955, 17; 1966–67, 11) (Ålin 79) (*AJA* 1961, no. 19).

**SKAPHIDIA:** In 1939 J. Sperling noted a prehistoric site on the Anemomylos hill south of the village (Sperling no. 35). Obsidian, EH sherds and some poor LH sherds have been found (*AJA* 1961, no. 2). Hellenistic statues and Roman tombs were found at 'Lavrion' (*AD* 23, 1968, *Chr.* 1, 162; 24, 1969, *Chr.* 1, 148).

**SKILLOUNTIA:** Just to the west of the village of Skillountia, formerly Mazi, a temple was discovered in 1880, and was partly excavated by Ph. Stavropoulos in 1938 (*AA* 1940, 235ff) (*AJA* 44, 1940, 539) and by N.

Zapheiropoulos in 1951 (*BCH* 1952, 223). N. Yialouris carried out further excavation in 1960. It is an early 4th century Doric temple. Fragments of the pediment sculptures have been recovered, which may have shown the battle of gods and giants (*PAE* 1960, 174ff) (*Ergon* 1960, 135ff). Yialouris suggests it is the temple of Skillountian Athena (*AD* 16, 1960, *Chr.* 135-36) (*BCH* 1961, 719ff). Another suggested identification is the temple of Artemis Daidaleia (Meyer 1957, 45f) (*BCH* 1962, 629) (*AD* 23, 1968, *Mel.* 291f).

In 1971 L. Parlama excavated a 4th century B.C. cemetery about 2 km northwest of the temple. There were three grave enclosures with 15 slab-covered graves (*AAA* 5, 1972, 206ff) (*BCH* 1973, 308).

For other remains in the area, see Makrisia.

**STREPHI:** N. Yialouris investigated a LH IIIB chamber tomb near Strephi (*AD* 17, 1961–62, *Chr.* 107) (*BCH* 1962, 743).

A. Khoremis has reported on excavations by the Alpheios. Traces of buildings with LH II sherds were uncovered, Classical graves and Hellenistic buildings (*AD* 23, 1968, *Chr.* 1, 171; 24, 1969, *Chr.* 1, 151f).

**THEISOA:** N. Yialouris examined two Hellenistic cist graves discovered during road works between Theisoa and Matesi in 1965. The tombs are divided into two levels by a grill of slabs inserted into the walls. Apparently each corpse was laid on the grill and fell into the lower chamber when decomposed (*AAA* 1, 1968, 189ff) (*AD* 21, 1966, *Chr.* 1, 172).

**TRYPITI:** A Classical and Hellenistic settlement has been noted on the hill at Trypiti, formerly Bitsibardi, south of the confluence of the Erymanthos and Alpheios Rivers. On the east side MH and LH sherds were noted (Sperling nos. 4-5) (Meyer 1957, 41) (*PAE* 1955, 242) (*AJA* 1961, no. 18).

**VRESTON:** N. Yialouris investigated the remains of an ancient city, perhaps ancient Pteleia, near Vreston. There are 4th century B.C. fortifications, a theatre and a cemetery (*PAE* 1955, 243-44) (Meyer 1957, 55ff,

71ff). Further Hellenistic and Roman remains were found in 1967 (*AD* 23, 1968, *Chr.* 1, 162).

**VRINA:** Two circular constructions were discovered near Vrina, south of Krestena. One contained numerous cist graves (5th century). Other cist graves were noted west of the village (*BCH* 1954, 130).

# Laconia

**ALESIA:** A. Delivorrias has reported a 1967 excavation of late Roman tombs at 'Ayios Georgios' by Alesia, south of Sparta (*AD* 23, 1968, *Chr.* 1, 152).

**AMYKLAI:** In 1889–90 Kh. Tsountas excavated the site of the ancient Amyklaion at the church of Ayia Kyriaki. He located the foundation of the throne of Amyklaion Apollo and a sacrificial area, and also noted prehistoric remains, including two Mycenaean chamber tombs somewhere in the vicinity (*PAE* 1889, 22; 1890, 36f) (*AE* 1892, 1ff). A. Furtwängler excavated in the prehistoric level in 1904, and after his death the Greek Archaeological Society under A. Skias completed his planned excavation in 1907 and removed the church from the top of the hill (*PAE* 1907, 104ff) (*Jahrbuch* 33, 1918, 109ff). In 1924 E. Buschor and W. von Massow carried out excavations, particularly in the prehistoric settlement on the southeast slopes of the hill. Pottery ranges from EH to LH IIIC, proto-Geometric, Geometric and then Archaic on. The site was definitely a sanctuary from the Archaic period onward. LH III psi-type figurines and wheel-made animal figurines were found, and while not definitely from a votive deposit, they indicate that there was a Mycenaean sanctuary here. The proto-Geometric and Geometric material is not necessarily of a votive character, but it is associated with the LH IIIC votive material rather than the Archaic material. Thus not only is Amyklai an exception to the general destruction at the end of the LH IIIB period in Laconia, but it is one of the very few places where there may have been cult continuity (*AM* 52, 1927, 1ff including history of previous work) (Desborough 42, 88f) (*BSA* 1960, 74ff).

In 1956 Kh. Khristou found a large votive hoard by the church of Ayia Paraskevi by the modern village of Amyklai (formerly Slavokhori). They range from the Geometric to Hellenistic periods; most are Archaic. There were a number of clay plaques with Laconian 'hero-reliefs'. They probably come from the shrine of Alexandra-Kassandra and Zeus-Agamemnon mentioned by Pausanias (III 19.6). In 1960–62 Khristou carried out trials in an unsuccessful attempt to locate the sanctuary itself. More votives were found however, including inscribed vases (*PAE* 1956, 211f; 1960, 228ff; 1961, 177f) (*Ergon* 1956, 100ff; 1960, 167ff; 1962, 133) (*AD* 18, 1963, *Chr.* 1, 86).

**ANGELONA:** In 1905 A. J. B. Wace and F. W. Hasluck of the British School excavated on the Kollyri plateau by Angelona on the Malea peninsula. They found Classical and Hellenistic votives and cult objects from a local heroon, including a statue base, a bronze snake, miniature vases and terracotta figurines (*BSA* 11, 1904–5, 81ff). A prehistoric site with EH and LH III pottery has been noted to the northeast (*BSA* 1961, 138) (*Gazetteer* no. 148).

**ANTHOKHORION:** In 1961–62 Kh. Khristou made soundings by the Analipsis church at Anthokhorion near Xerokambi south of Sparta. Mycenaean and Geometric levels were identified, an Archaic deposit with lead figurines, and Classical and later layers (*AD* 17, 1961–62, *Chr.* 84-85; 18, 1963, *Chr.* 1, 86) (*PAE* 1962, 113ff) (*Ergon* 1962, 134f) (*Gazetteer* no. 100).

**APHYSION:** In 1963 Kh. Khristou excavated a rectangular Classical building at 'Ktirakia' by Aphysi between Sparta and Khrysapha. In late Roman times it was converted into a tomb and an apse was added in the Byzantine period. Fragments of reliefs of the Flavian period were found in a pit within the apse (*PAE* 1963, 130ff) (*Ergon* 1963, 102ff). A Roman and later house had been noted previously (*AD* 17, 1961–62, *Chr.* 84).

**ARKINES:** Two small and poorly constructed tholoi were excavated at the head of the Goranoi river by Kh. Tsountas in 1889 and G. Sotiriadis in 1910 (*AE* 1889, 132ff) (*PAE* 1889, 122; 1910, 277). In 1960 a prehistoric settlement was noted on the Paizoulia hill to the northeast of the tholoi (*BSA* 1961, 128ff) (cf. *BSA* 16, 1909–10, 66-67). The site is unusual for its remoteness and height, and its importance is that it lay on a route over Taygetos (*Gazetteer* no. 101).

**ARNA:** By Arna, on the east slopes of southern Taygetos, Kh. Tsountas reported 'Hellenic' graves in 1889 (*AE* 1889, 133ff) (cf. *BSA* 16, 1909–10, 67).

**ASTERI:** At Asteri, southeast of Skala near the mouth of the Eurotas, Lord William Taylour, R. Hope Simpson and D. French carried out a trial excavation in 1959. Sherds of EH, MH, including gray Minyan and matt-painted ware, LH I–II, LH IIIA–B and possibly IIIC sherds were found, but the site was much denuded (*BSA* 1960, 89; 67, 1972, 262f). Other prehistoric sites were noted in the Asteri area (*BSA* 1960, 89, 92; 1961, 165).

**AYIOS STEPHANOS:** In 1959 Lord William Taylour and R. Hope Simpson made a trial excavation on the Ayios Stephanos hill, southwest of Skala, and Lord William Taylour returned to excavate the site in 1960 and 1963, and again in 1973–74. The site was occupied from EH to LH IIIB period when it was probably abandoned, as there was little evidence for destruction or burning. The settlement was important during the transitional MH/LH I period. Study of the pottery from the site has shown contact with Crete from the MM period onward. There is strong evidence of Minoan influence on the local painted pottery in a period corresponding to MM IIIB to LM IA; there is much similarity with the material from Kastri on Kythera. Over 100 burials were found within the settlement ranging from EH to LH IIIB. Many could not be dated, as grave goods were rare (*BSA* 1960, 97ff) (*AD* 16, 1960, *Chr.* 104f; 19, 1964, *Chr.* 1, 146ff) (*BSA* 67, 1972, 205ff) (*AR* 1973–74, 15ff; 1974–75, 15ff).

**AYIOS VASILIOS:** South of Sparta, southeast of the junction of the main highway and the road to Xerokambi, by the ruined Ayios Nikolaos chapel, Classical and later pottery, fragments of columns and of Hellenistic and Roman statues were noted; and well as EH, MH and copious Mycenaean sherds (*BSA* 1960, 80ff).

**ELAPHONISOS ISLAND:** Abundant indications of EH and LH settlement were noted on Elaphonisi by Kh. Khristou and R. Hope Simpson (*AR* 1957, 10) (*BSA* 1961, 145ff). N. C. Fleming of the National Institute of Oceanography at Cambridge noted submerged prehistoric remains in 1967 in the strait between the island and the mainland and the Pavlopetri islet. An expedition from Cambridge University led by R. C. Jones, with A. Harding, G. Cadogan and R. Howell examined these remains in 1968. MH and LH pottery and walls as well as Roman and Byzantine material were found on Elaphonisi, once joined to the mainland. The remains in the channel appear to be mostly Mycenaean. Houses and streets and more than 30 cist graves were planned. One apsidal building is probably EH. An extensive Mycenaean cemetery was noted on the shore of the mainland, some of which it was mentioned that A. Delivorrias has since excavated (*BSA* 64, 1969, 113ff) (*AR* 1967–68, 10; 1968–69, 17) (*Science Journal*, April 1968, 51ff).

**EPIDAUROS LIMERA:** The site of Epidauros Limera, reputed to be a foundation from the Argive Epidauros, is located on the coast about 5 km north of Monemvasia. Classical and later remains have been noted (Frazer, *Pausanias* 3, 387) (Wace and Hasluck, *BSA* 14, 1907–8, 179ff) and in a surface investigation in 1957 sherds of possibly Neolithic and LH I–IIIC as well as Classical and Hellenistic material were found (*BSA* 1961, 136ff) (*Gazetteer* no. 146). At 'Ayia Triada' to the southwest of the acropolis two Mycenaean tombs with LH IIIB–C vases were explored by Kh. Khristou in 1956. Mycenaean tombs were also excavated by Khristou around Ayios Ioannis village west of Epidauros Limera (*PAE* 1956, 207ff) (*Ergon* 1956, 96ff). A small prehistoric settlement was noted about one km northeast of Ayios Ioannis with EH–LH III sherds (*Gazetteer* no. 147) (Desborough 89).

**GERAKI:** In 1905 A. J. B. Wace and F. W. Hasluck carried out a trial exca-

vation on the site of Classical Geronthrai at Geraki in an attempt to locate buildings mentioned by Pausanias (III 22.6-7). While they identified
none of these they found three MH cist graves and traces of an EH–LH III
settlement. Some walls on the acropolis are probably Mycenaean, and
may be MH (*BSA* 11, 1904–5, 91ff; 16, 1909–10, 72ff) (*Gazetteer* no. 105).

**GORITSA:** In the Tsaltas ravine by Goritsa, southeast of Sparta, von
Vacano found evidence of Neolithic habitation in a double cave (*AA*
1942, 156). An EH–LH III settlement has been noted nearby (*BSA* 1960,
83).

**GYTHEION:** A. Skias investigated Gytheion, excavated the theatre and
made smaller excavations throughout the city in 1891 (*PAE* 1891, 27ff;
71ff) (*AE* 1892, 185ff). Little of the ancient city remains due to modern
building. For a discussion of ancient topography see E. S. Forster (*BSA*
10, 1903–4, 179ff; 13, 1906–7, 219ff). A Temple of Augustus was acci-
dently discovered and excavated in 1923. The inscriptions have been
published by S. Kougeas (*Ellenika* 1, 1928, 7ff) (*BCH* 1923, 511). Late Roman houses have been excavated (*AD* 21, 1966, *Chr.* 1, 157) and a late
Roman family tomb at 'Selinitsa' (*AD* 23, 1968, *Chr.* 1, 152f).

**KALYVIA PELLANES:** In 1927 Th. Karakhalios conducted trials on the
Palaiokastro hill to the northeast of the village and found some Mycenaean material. He also excavated a Mycenaean chamber tomb to the north of
the hill at 'Spilies'. K. Romaios excavated another (*AR* 1926–27, 257) (*AD*
10, 1926, *par.* 41ff) (*BSA* 1961, 125ff).

**KALYVIA TIS SOKHAS:** A. von Prott located the site of the Eleusinion
mentioned by Pausanias (III 20.5) (*AM* 29, 1904, 1ff). R. M. Dawkins excavated in 1910 and found material from the temple, but not the actual
foundations (*BSA* 16, 1909–10, 12ff). In 1947 a flood partially washed out
the site and revealed a number of ancient blocks. The British School put
the site in order and carried out some minor excavation in 1949 (*AR*
1947–48, 39f; 1948–49, 5) (*BSA* 45, 1950, 261ff; 47, 1952, 118ff).

**KERIA:** At Keria near Kounos in southwest Mani A. Delivorrias has examined various ancient remains from churches including a very elaborate Hellenistic naiskos-tombstone (*AAA* 1, 1968, 119ff).

**KIPOULA:** Kipoula, near Kounos in southwest Mani is probably the site of ancient Hippola (Frazer, *Pausanias* 3, 399). Geometric to Hellenistic material has been noted (*BSA* 13, 1906–7, 244f).

**KOTRONAS:** Ancient Teuthrone (Pausanias III 21. 7; 25.4) is located on the Skopa promontory by Kotronas. Various Hellenistic to Roman remains were noted by E. S. Forster (*BSA* 13, 1906–7, 256-57) and C. Le Roy (*BCH* 1961, 215ff). EH pottery, a pithos burial, and possibly MH and LH sherds have been found (*BSA* 1961, 119) and a Roman bath complex reported (*AD* 23, 1968, *Chr.* 1, 153ff).

**KOUPHOVOUNO:** von Vacano excavated Neolithic and EH houses and graves in 1942 on the Kouphovouno hill about 2 km southwest of Sparta, southeast of the road to Ayios Ioannis. No details were published (*AA* 1942, 156). In a surface study by R. Hope Simpson in 1957 no MH or LH I–II and only a few LH III sherds were found. The site was most important in the Neolithic and EH periods (*BSA* 1960, 72-73). K. Dimakopoulou has reported more Neolithic and EH finds (*AD* 21, 1966, *Chr.* 1, 158).

**KRANAI:** On Kranai, the island off Gytheion from which Helen and Paris were said to have sailed, an extensive Mycenaean settlement with some possible EH habitation was noted (*BSA* 1961, 114) (*Gazetteer* no. 124).

**KROKEAI:** The ruins of Classical Krokeai at 'Alai-Bey' by modern Krokeai and the nearby Lapis Lacedaemonius mines have been described by Frazer (Frazer, *Pausanias* 3, 374-75), H. A. Ormerod (*BSA* 16,

1909–10, 68ff) and C. Le Roy (*BCH* 1961, 206ff). On the Karneos hill south of Krokeai a plundered LH II–III tomb was investigated in 1955 and traces of others noted (*BCH* 1956, 277) (*BSA* 1960, 104f) (*Gazetteer* no. 121).

**LAGIO:** A number of remains have been noted in the area of Lagio. At 'Glyphada' on the shore south of Lagio, northeast of Gytheion, remains of Roman houses were noted by E. S. Forster (*BSA* 13, 1906–7, 230). On the Paizoulia hill north of this, EH, MH, and LH II–III pottery has been found, and to the south and east of the hill Classical and Roman sherds and remains of a large probably Roman building. Another prehistoric settlement was noted nearer Lagio (*BSA* 1960, 104ff) (*Gazetteer* nos. 122-23).

**LAS:** Classical Las is probably located on the hill of the Medieval Castle of Passava. Classical and Hellenistic sherds are abundant. The citadel is perhaps also the Homeric Las, although nothing Mycenaean has been found (Frazer, *Pausanias* 3, 392) (*BSA* 12, 1905–6, 274ff; 13, 1906–7, 232ff).

**MAGOULA:** Trial pits dug at Magoula by the British School produced Archaic to Roman material including Archaic stelae (*BSA* 16, 1909–10, 3; 1960, 82). A Hellenistic mosaic was found in Magoula in 1915, showing Tritons and sea monsters (*AD* 4, 1918, 171).

**MAVROVOUNI:** At 'Stena' 3 km southwest of Gytheion toward Mavrovouni, proto-Geometric sherds and part of an iron weapon were found by Kh. Khristou (*AR* 1956, 12) (*BSA* 1961, 115). EH–LH III sherds, Mycenaean chamber tombs, Classical to Roman pottery and tombs have been noted by Mavrovouni village (*BSA* 1960, 117ff) (*Gazetteer* no. 125).

**MENELAION:** The sanctuary of Menelaus, the Menelaion, on the heights above the Eurotas east of Sparta, was first excavated by Ludwig

Ross in 1833–34. The remains consist of three platforms on which a small probably 5th century building or altar stood. A large number of small flat lead and clay figurines were found (L. Ross, *Archäologische Aufsätze* 1861, 2, 341ff). In 1889 Kh. Tsountas and P. Kastriotis completed the excavation of the Menelaion and found more lead figurines. The sanctuary probably goes back to the Laconian Geometric period. Some Mycenaean sherds were also found at this time (*AE* 1889, 130f) (Frazer, *Pausanias* 3, 360). In 1909–10 the British School under R. M. Dawkins excavated a large Mycenaean house and other Mycenaean remains on the hill (*BSA* 15, 1908–9, 108ff; 16, 1909–10, 4ff). After more than 50 years, the British School under H. W. Catling returned to the site in 1973 to excavate in the Mycenaean settlement. Some MH and LH IIA sherds were found without associated buildings. An LH IIB–IIIA1 complex of buildings was excavated. It was partly covered by the house excavated by Dawkins, but the entire area was abandoned before LH IIIA2. The house was reoccupied in LH IIIB2 and destroyed by fire at the end of the IIIB period. Work continued in 1974 (*AR* 1973–74, 14f; 1974–75, 12ff).

**NEAPOLIS:** Ancient Boiai was north of the modern city of Neapolis (Vatika). Only a few remains have been noted (Frazer, *Pausanias* 3, 384) (Wace and Hasluck, *BSA* 14, 1907–8, 168ff). Remains of a Roman bath have been excavated in Neapolis (*AD* 25, 1970, *Chr.* 1, 172; 26, 1971, *Chr.* 1, 120ff).

**OITYLOS:** Modern Oitylos, north of Areopolis, is the site of ancient Oitylos. For a description of remains, see E. S. Forster (*BSA* 10, 1903–4, 160-61). Kh. Khristou has noted an ancient wall built into the church of Ayia Marina (*AR* 1957, 10). Some possibly LH ware has been found (*BSA* 1961, 121).

**PHOINIKI:** Near Phoiniki east of Asopos on the Malea peninsula inscribed stones and over 70 bronze tablets relating to the sanctuary of Apollo Hyperteleatas have been found. Th. Sophoulis excavated in 1885 in an unsuccessful attempt to locate the temple itself (*AE* 1884, 79ff, 197ff; 1885, 58ff) (*PAE* 1885, 31ff) (Frazer, *Pausanias* 3, 383) (cf. *BSA* 14, 1907–8, 165; 24, 1919–21, 137). In 1968 the discovery of an Archaic cap-

ital led to the excavation of the foundations of a building which is probably the temple. Sixth to fifth century vases were found (*AD* 24, 1969,
*Chr.* 1, 138ff).

**PLYTRA:** On the Goulas hill about 2 km northwest of Plytra over Zyli
Bay, sherds of Neolithic through LH III periods have been found, as well
as Classical sherds and the foundations of small buildings. This is probably the site of the 'Parakyparissioi Achaioi' mentioned by Pausanias (III
22.9) with a temple of Athena Kyparissia on the summit. By Pausanias'
day the population had presumably moved down to Plytra, ancient
Asopos, where Roman inscriptions, tombs and houses have been noted
(Frazer, *Pausanias* 3, 382f) (Wace and Hasluck, *BSA* 14, 1907–8, 163ff;
1961, 139ff) (*AR* 1956, 12).

**PYRGOS:** In 1958 Mr. and Mrs. A. Petrokheilou discovered skulls and
Neolithic sherds in the Alepotrypa cave, one of the three Diros caves on
the bay below Pyrgos in the Mani (*Kathimerini* Dec. 3, 1959) (*AR* 1959,
11), and they later carried out further researches. Pottery, stone and obsidian tools, shells and a silver bracelet, and two primitive statuettes
were among the finds (*AR* 1961–62, 10) (*Kathimerini* Nov. 12, 1961; April
18, 1962). G. Papathanasopoulos excavated in 1970 and 1971. The cave
was inhabited throughout the late Neolithic period. Hearths, storage
pits, pottery, spearheads and burials were found. The cave was apparently blocked by an earthquake, accounting for the abundant skeletal
material in it. He also investigated the other caves and found evidence of
widespread Neolithic occupation outside the caves around the bay (*AAA*
1, 1968, 83ff; 4, 1971, 12ff, 289ff).

**SKOURA:** Chance finds of an ancient wall and a Doric capital were reported from Skoura (*BCH* 1960, 693) (*AR* 1959, 9). In 1966 K. Dimakopoulou excavated a group of five plundered Mycenaean chamber tombs
about 2 km north of the village at 'Melathria'. Vases of LH IIIA–B date and
three phi-type figurines were found (*AAA* 1, 1968, 37ff) (*AD* 22, 1967, *Chr.*
1, 197ff).

**SKOUTARI:** At 'Dikhova' or 'Kamaresi' between Skoutari and Agerano south of Gytheion, A. Delivorrias reported the excavation of a late Archaic shrine of Aphrodite and a late Roman basilica (*AD* 23, 1968, *Chr.* 1, 153; 24, 1969, *Chr.* 1, 141).

**SPARTA:** Classical Sparta consisted of a loose grouping of villages around the acropolis. There were few monumental buildings and the city was not fortified until the early 3rd century B.C. At the southwest corner of the acropolis the remains of the theatre have long been visible. The American School under C. Waldstein carried out some excavations in 1892–93. The building known as the tomb of Leonidas was excavated. It is probably a small Hellenistic temple. The theatre was partly excavated, and a circular platform with a pedestal in the center (*AJA* 8, 1893, 335ff; 410ff; 9, 1894, 545ff). For a description of these excavations and other remains known from Sparta, see Frazer (Frazer, *Pausanias* 3, 322ff). See also H. Dressel and A. Milchhöfer ("Die antiken Kunstwerke aus Sparta und Umgebung," *AM* 2, 1877, 393ff), and the catalogue prepared by M. N. Tod and A. J. B. Wace (*Catalogue of the Sparta Museum*, Oxford 1906).

In 1906 the British School began a series of important excavations at Sparta which continued until 1910. Those taking part included R. C. Bosanquet, A. J. B. Wace, G. Dickens, R. M. Dawkins, H. J. W. Tillyard, R. Traquair, A. M. Woodward and J. P. Droop. The sanctuary of Athena Chalkioikos (Brazen-House) was located behind the theatre; Geometric pottery was found. More excavation was carried out in the theatre. The ancient city walls were traced, and some Hellenistic graves were excavated.

The most important discovery of this series of excavations was the site of the precinct of Artemis Orthia. Part of what had been thought to be a Roman circus by the Eurotas (cf. Frazer, *Pausanias* 3, 325) turned out to be a semicircular amphitheatre built in the 2nd century A.D. around the altar in front of the Artemis Orthia temple for viewing the ritual flogging of Spartan youths; remains of Classical houses underlay the amphitheatre. The present temple, rebuilt in the Hellenistic period, rests on 6th century foundations. This partly lay over remains of an earlier temple. The earliest sanctuary consisted of a walled enclosure and an altar. A series of altars dating from the Archaic period or perhaps earlier down to the Roman period was found. An enormous number of votives going back to the Geometric period were recovered including a large number of lead figurines (*BSA* 12, 1905–6, 277ff; 13, 1906–7, 1ff; 14, 1907–8, 1ff; 15, 1908–9, 1ff; 16, 1909–10, 1ff) (R. M. Dawkins et al., *The Sanctuary of Artemis Orthia*

*at Sparta, JHS* Suppl. no. 5, London 1929). The excavators believed that
the sanctuary existed from the 9th or even the 10th century B.C., and that a
layer of sand put down over the Archaic level provided a *terminus post
quem* for the present temple of about 600 B.C. These dates have been questioned. It is maintained that hardly anything at the site is earlier than the
8th century, that the Geometric material may continue to c. 650 B.C., and
that the sand layer may be as late as 540 B.C. (On this controversy see:
*Gnomon* 9, 1933, 1ff) (*JHS* 50, 1930, 329ff) (*BSA* 58, 1963, 1ff.)

The British School resumed excavation in 1924 under A. M. Wood-
ward and work continued until 1928. These excavations were concentrated on the theatre and acropolis. A votive deposit from the sanctuary of
Athena Chalkioikos from the Geometric to Hellenistic periods was found.
The stage area of the theatre was completely cleared and some of the
seats. The earliest structural remains are probably Augustan. Various late
Roman houses, and a bathing establishment or large villa were excavated.
A small sanctuary, of the 7th century B.C. at the earliest, was uncovered
with votives with the name Athena inscribed on them. Some LH III
sherds were also found on the acropolis (*BSA* 26, 1923–25, 116ff; 27, 1925–
26, 173ff; 28, 1926–27, 1ff; 29, 1927–28, 1ff; 30, 1928–30, 151ff).

In 1949 the British School excavated on behalf of the Greek Department of Antiquities on the site of the modern stadium, between the
modern town and the acropolis, where Ph. Stavropoulos had already
done some work. Some late Roman buildings were excavated and some
Mycenaean sherds were also found (*BSA* 45, 1950, 282ff).

Kh. Khristou carried out further excavation in the stadium in 1957
and found traces of occupation going back to the 7th century B.C. and a
few more Mycenaean sherds (*AR* 1957, 10). Since 1960 Khristou has
been working in Sparta in various places. He resumed the unfinished
clearing of the theatre, excavated a small shrine in the suburb of Kalo-
gonia, a large Hellenistic altar-like structure in the Psychiko suburb, and
various Archaic burials. On the Acropolis he re-examined the 'Round
building' and found a hearth and pit in it (*PAE* 1960, 232; 1961, 179; 1962,
113ff; 1964, 102ff; 1965, 97f) (*Ergon* 1960, 173; 1962, 133ff; 1964, 102ff) (*AD*
16, 1960, *Chr.* 102; 17, 1961–62, *Chr.* 83f; 19, 1964, *Mel.* 123ff; 19, 1964,
*Chr.* 1, 135ff).

Th. Karageorga, K. Dimakopoulou and A. Delivorrias have carried
out various rescue operations in the city, including a Roman villa south
of the theatre with mosaic floors, and a Roman bath with mosaics 500 m
southwest of the acropolis (*AD* 19, 1964, *Chr.* 1, 144f; 20, 1965, *Chr.* 1,
170ff). North of the Artemis Orthia sanctuary an unidentified shrine,
probably a heroon, was excavated between 1966 and 1968. Classical pottery and tiles were recovered, two comic masks, and an Archaic hero re-

lief (*AAA* 1, 1968, 41ff) (*AD* 22, 1967, *Chr.* 1, 200ff; 23, 1968, *Chr.* 1, 151-52; 24, 1969, *Chr.* 1, 131ff).

**CAPE TAINARON:** For a description of Cape Tainaron and early finds there, see Frazer (Frazer, *Pausanias* 3, 396ff). A collection of bronze statuettes of bulls and horses found in 1856 is probably a votive deposit from the shrine of Poseidon. The site was re-examined by the British School (*BSA* 13, 1906–7, 249ff; 1961, 123ff).

**TSASI:** Th. Karakhalios excavated a Mycenaean chamber tomb about 500 m east of the village sometime before W.W. II. LH IIIA–B vases were recovered, but the tomb was not published (*AJA* 42, 1938, 539). A settlement with EH and LH sherds was noted on the hill above (*BSA* 1960, 92ff) (*Gazetteer* no. 115).

**VAPHIO:** In 1889 Kh. Tsountas excavated a tholos tomb at Vaphio south of Sparta. The tomb had been partly plundered, but an unplundered grave pit of probably LH II date was found. In addition to the gold 'Vaphio cups', gems, pottery and an axehead with two holes were found (*AE* 1888, 197ff; 1889, 136ff). Conservation work was done on the tomb in 1962 (*AD* 18, 1963, *Chr.* 1, 87).

On the Palaiopyrgi hill nearby, an extensive prehistoric settlement has been noted, with EH and LH pottery, LH IIIB pottery being particularly abundant (*BSA* 1960, 76ff).

**XEROKAMBI:** Xerokambi, south of Sparta, is possibly the site of ancient Harpleia. There is a polygonal bridge, probably Hellenistic. For a description of this area, see H. von Prott (*AM* 19, 1904, 13f) (cf. *BSA* 1960, 82).

**ZARAX:** Limen Ierakas north of Monemvasia is the site of ancient Zarax, destroyed by the time of Pausanias. The few ancient remains have been described by A. J. B. Wace and F. W. Hasluck (*BSA* 15, 1908–9, 158ff). A terracotta figurine somewhat similar to the Venus de Milo has been published from a tomb (*AE* 1908, 135).

# Messenia

Those interested in the archaeology and history of Messenia should turn to a book entitled *The Minnesota Messenia Expedition* (hereafter abbreviated as *UMME*), edited by William A. McDonald and George E. Rapp Jr., published in 1972 by the University of Minnesota Press, Minneapolis, Minn. This expedition has been a multi-disciplinary research project that has continued for almost 15 years. Authors contributing to the Minnesota Press volume include Stanley Aschenbrenner, John Chadwick, Strathmore R. B. Cooke, Jesse E. Fant, Eiler Henrickson, Richard Hope Simpson, John F. Lazenby, William G. Loy, Fred E. Lukermann, William A. McDonald, Frederick R. Matson, Catherine Nobeli, George R. Rapp, Jr., Peter Topping, Herman J. Van Wersch, H. E. Wright, Jr. and N. J. Yassoglou.

**AKOVITIKA (Kalamon):** In 1958 at Akovitika west of Kalamata, N. Yialouris excavated buildings of Hellenistic and Roman date and found a group of Geometric and Archaic statuettes including two small bronze kouroi. Excavation was stopped due to high water level (*BCH* 1959, 639ff) (*AR* 1959, 11) (cf. *AM* 83, 1968, 175ff). In 1969 excavations were carried out by P. Themelis and Th. Karageorga which revealed a huge EH megaron type building (35 m by 15 m) and associated buildings. A second large building was uncovered in 1970. They were of EH II date, perhaps with some MH reoccupation (*AAA* 3, 1970, 303ff) (*AD* 25, 1970, *Chr.* 1, 177ff; 26, 1971, *Chr.* 1, 126ff). To the south of this, a sanctuary of Poseidon was uncovered. It was destroyed in the late 7th century and rebuilt. The statuettes found in 1958 were probably votives from this shrine (*AAA* 2, 1969, 359ff) (*AD* 1970, *Chr.* 1, 177ff).

**ANDANIA (Messinis):** The site of ancient Andania was identified at 'Elliniko', about 2 km east of Desylla village (renamed Andania) on the east side of the upper Messenian plain. M. N. Valmin more plausibly identified Andania with the site at 'Ayios Athanasios' by the Divari spring by Konstantinoi on the west side of the plain (Valmin 1930, 91ff) (*Bull. Lund* 1928–29, 32ff). It was here that the inscription regulating the Andanian mysteries was found (*IG* V.1. 1390). There are ruins of buildings and walls and evidence of Classical to Roman occupation (F. Hiller von Gärtringen and H. Latterman, *Hira und Andania, Einundsiebzigstes Programm sum Winckelmannsfeste,* Berlin 1911) (Roebuck 7ff). Andania was also once identified at Trypha where A. Lykakis excavated a Roman mosaic with a hunting scene he believed depicted the mysteries (*PAE* 1900, 17).

**ANO KOPANAKI (Triphylias):** At 'Akourthi' about 1.5 km west of the village, between the highway and the railway, are the remains of three tholoi. M. N. Valmin partially excavated one, and fully excavated another in 1927. It was in use in the LH II–III periods and there was evidence of a later cult in the tomb (*Bull. Lund* 1927–28, 31ff) (Valmin 1930, 79ff) (*UMME* no. 234). About one km northeast of the village on the Stylari hill are remains of a Classical settlement and Hellenistic fortification. LH II–III sherds have been noted (Valmin 1930, 79ff) (*UMME* no. 233).

**ANTHEIA (Kalamon):** The Ellinika ridge runs north and south, east of Antheia village (formerly Beïsage). At 'Palaiokastro' on the north end of the ridge are the remains of Classical Thouria. For early bibliography and a description of the site, see Frazer (Frazer, *Pausanias* 3, 424ff). The Classical site has also been investigated by A. Skias (*AE* 1911, 117f) and M. N. Valmin (Valmin 1930, 56ff) (*Bull. Lund* 1928–29, 1ff). Skias also noted remains of numerous Mycenaean chamber tombs on the east slopes of the ridge. R. Hope Simpson and R. Howell explored the area to the northeast of Aitheia village (south of Antheia village) and the ridge.

They located an EH settlement and an MH–LM settlement, and noted at least 26 chamber tombs (*BSA* 1957, 243f; 1966, 121ff) (*AJA* 1961, 1964, 1969, no. 78) (*UMME* no. 137). Proto-Geometric vases are reported from a tomb on the site (*AD* 20, 1965, *Chr.* 2, 207). The Classical city and some of the Mycenaean chamber tombs were also investigated by N. Yialouris (*AR* 1959, 11; 1960, 11) (*BCH* 1959, 640f).

**ARTEMISIA (Kalamon):** The chapel of the Panagia at 'Volimos' about 5 km northwest of Artemisia (formerly Sternitsa) is the probable location of the shrine of Artemis Limnatis mentioned by Pausanias (IV 4.2; 31.3) (*BCH* 1959, 640) (*AJA* 1961, 255) (*BSA* 1966, 121). For alternate locations, see M. N. Valmin (Valmin 1930, 182ff) and the discussion by C. A. Roebuck (Roebuck 118ff).

**AYIOS ANDREAS (Pylias):** Ph. Versakis excavated the site of the temple of Apollo Korythos at Ayios Andreas near Longa. He uncovered a number of buildings including four he identified as temples of various date. Material from Archaic and later periods was recovered (*AD* 2, 1916, 65ff). M. N. Valmin further explored the site, finding more inscriptions (*Bull. Lund* 1928–29, 39f, 146ff) (Valmin 1930, 174ff).

**AYIOS PHLOROS (Kalamon):** In 1929 M. N. Valmin discovered a small temple on the north side of the village, which he excavated in 1933. Inscriptions identify it as the shrine of the river god Pamisos mentioned by Pausanias (IV 3.10; 31.4). Finds date from Archaic to Roman times (Valmin 1938, 417ff).

**DIAVOLITSA (Messinis):** A Mycenaean chamber tomb was discovered by workmen in 1963 by the railroad station. LH IIIB pottery was recovered (*AD* 19, 1964, *Chr.* 1, 154). A Mycenaean settlement was noted on the Loutses hill about 800 m southwest of the village (*AJA* 1964, 1969, no. 31 C) (*UMME* no. 214).

**ELAIOKHORIO (Kalamon):** On the hill of the Ayioi Taxiarkhi chapel,

by Elaiokhorio (formerly Giannitza) are remains of Classical and Hellenistic fortifications and house walls. It is most likely the site of ancient
Kalamai, though it has also been identified as Pharai. Modern Kalamata
is more likely the site of Pharai. E. Pernice and O. Kern explored the
area in 1891, noting inscriptions and possible routes over Taygetos.
They identified the site as Pharai, as M. N. Valmin later did (*AM* 19,
1894, 351ff) (Valmin 1930, 40ff) (Roebuck 122ff) (Frazer, *Pausanias* 3,
421ff).

At Perivolakia about one km north of Giannitza, inscriptions men-
tioning Kalamai were found, and other antiquities were noted at 'Marmara' about 500 m northwest, by A. Skias (*AE* 1911, 117). R. Howell and R.
Hope Simpson noted a small LH III settlement at 'Sola' (*BSA* 1966, 119)
(*AJA* 1969, no. 79 C) (*UMME* no. 140).

**EXOKHIKON (Pylias):** A small destroyed tholos tomb was reported on
the Mistopholaka ridge near this village north of Kaplani in southern
Messenia. An LH IIIB stirrup jar was found (*AD* 20, 1965, *Chr.* 2, 208).
MH and LH sherds were noted on a settlement site on the Ayios Nikolaos ridge (*AJA* 1969, no. 73 A) (*UMME* no. 78).

**IKLAINA (Pylias):** In 1954 S. Marinatos conducted a trial excavation at
'Traganes' about 1.5 km west of the village. He uncovered part of an LH
III building with pebble floors and fragments of frescoes and noted an-
other rectangular building nearby (*PAE* 1954, 308ff) (*Ergon* 1954, 42) (*AJA*
1961, no. 52) (*UMME* no. 46). An MH pithos has been reported from
Iklaina (*AR* 1961, 10).

**KALAMATA:** Modern Kalamata probably occupies the site of ancient
Pharai, and substantial ancient remains are few (Valmin 1930, 45ff) (Roebuck 122ff). On the Kastro of Kalamata, LH III and Archaic to Roman
sherds have been noted. N. Yialouris has suggested that some of the
walls on the Kastro may be Mycenaean, and he has reported various
antiquities from the area of the ancient city, which lay to the south and
east of the Kastro (*BCH* 1959, 632ff) (*AR* 1959, 11; 1960, 11). G. Papathanasopoulos reported a Geometric pithos burial found in 1961 (*AD* 17,
1961–62, *Chr.* 96) and Roman graves were found in 1967 (*AD* 23, 1968,

*Chr.* 1, 156). On the Tourles hill about 500 m northeast of the Kastro remains of Mycenaean chamber tombs and probably also of a Mycenaean settlement were noted by R. Hope Simpson; as well as LH III sherds, some possibly EH sherds were found, and traces of Classical occupation (*BSA* 1957, 242ff; 1966, 116ff).

**KALYVIA (Messinis):** A Mycenaean chamber tomb was destroyed by bulldozers south of the village in 1966. LH IIIB vases were recovered *(AD* 22, 1967, *Chr.* 1, 206). A Mycenaean site was noted on the Pano Khorio hill 300 m east of the village (*AJA* 1969, no. 33A) *UMME* no. 210).

**KAMBOS (Kalamon):** In 1891 Kh. Tsountas excavated a fine tholos tomb about one km west of Kambos, southeast of Kalamata. The tomb had been robbed in antiquity, but LH II–III material was found and two statuettes of Cretan MM III type (*PAE* 1891, 23) (*AE* 1891, 189ff) (*UMME* no. 146). On the Zarnata hill to the southwest of the village are remains of a Venetian fort, perhaps with Classical foundations. It is probably the site of ancient Gerenia. Classical and Hellenistic sherds have been found (Valmin 1930, 182ff). S. Kougeas explored the area in 1932. He identified some walls as prehistoric which are probably Classical at the earliest. In the Kotoulas caves about 3.5 km southwest he found Neolithic pottery (*Ellenika* 6, 1933, 261ff) (cf. *BSA* 1957, 237ff).

**KARDAMYLI (Kalamon):** The acropolis of Homeric and later Kardamyli lies about one km northeast of the modern village. Remains of Archaic, Classical and later periods have been noted (*BSA* 10, 1903–4, 163) (*Bull. Lund* 1928–29, 42ff) (Valmin 1930, 198ff) (*BCH* 1959, 639) (*AD* 22, 1967, *Chr.* 1, 206). Mycenaean sherds have also been reported (*BSA* 1957, 234ff) (*AD* 20, 1965, *Chr.* 2, 208).

**KARPOPHORA (Pylias):** A Bronze Age settlement had been noted on the Nichoria ridge by Karpophora and Rizomylo villages (*BSA* 1957, 249) and in 1959 N. Yialouris and W. McDonald conducted trials on the ridge, finding LH I–IIIB pottery and noting several tholos tombs (*ILN*

April 30, 1960, 740ff) (*BCH* 1960, 700) (*AJA* 1961, 1964, 1969, no. 76) (*UMME* no. 100) (*AR* 1959, 12; 1960, 11). In subsequent years N. Yialouris, G. Papathanasopoulos, A. Khoremis and Th. Karageorga carried out various excavations in cemeteries of all periods from Mycenaean to Roman. Particularly important were the Mycenaean chamber tomb cemeteries to the west, north and southeast of the ridge; the six tholoi on the ridge and below its northwest edge; the proto-Geometric cemetery one-half km to the north, and a proto-Geometric tholos (*AD* 16, 1960, *Chr.* 108; 17, 1961–62, *Chr.* 95f; 23, 1968, *Chr.* 1, 158f; 25, 1970, *Chr.* 1, 179ff; 26, 1971, *Chr.* 1, 129) (*AAA* 1, 1968, 205ff) (*AE* 1973, 25ff). The Nichoria ridge was excavated by the University of Minnesota Messenia Expedition under W. McDonald between 1969 and 1973. The site was inhabited from EH to sub-Mycenaean, proto-Geometric, Geometric and sporadically thereafter. It was an important site which would have controlled the ancient road to Pylos (*Hesperia* 41, 1972, 218ff; 44, 1975, 69ff) (*AD* 25, 1970, *Chr.* 1, 183ff; 26, 1971, *Chr.* 1, 131ff) (cf. Desborough 95f).

**KHANDRINOS (Pylias):** Within Khandrinos village on the Kalamata-Pylos road, N. Yialouris noted remains of ancient buildings and Archaic and Classical sherds. A group of Neolithic tools had previously been found (*AR* 1959, 11; 1960, 11). An Archaic pithos was reported (*AD* 19, 1964, *Chr.* 1, 149) and LH IIIB sherds noted by the Platania spring (*AJA* 1961, no. 67) (*UMME* no. 33).

At 'Kissos' about one km east of the village S. Marinatos excavated a tumulus with a number of pithoi and slab-lined cist graves with poor finds of LH IIIA–B date (*Ergon* 1966, 105ff) (*PAE* 1966, 121ff) (*AJA* 1969, no. 67 A) (*UMME* no. 32). At 'Koube' and 'Alonia' by the main road about 1.5 km west of Khandrinos, Yialouris noted two burial mounds with LH IIIB sherds (*AR* 1960, 11) (*AJA* 1961, no. 66) (*UMME* no. 37).

**KHAROKOPIO (Pylias):** In 1958 S. Marinatos cleared a Mycenaean tholos tomb by the Demotic School of Kharokopio, northwest of Koroni. It had previously been plundered (*PAE* 1958, 192f) (*Ergon* 1958, 154). He also noted traces of Classical and later buildings, the remains of what is probably a Roman bath, and Mycenaean sherds in the vicinity (*AR* 1958, 10; 1960, 11) (*AJA* 1961, 1964, no. 74) (*UMME* no. 109).

**KHORA (Triphylias):** The partnership of C. W. Blegen of the University of Cincinnati and K. Kourouniotis for the purpose of exploring western Messenia was originally formed in 1927–28, but it was not until 1939 that the first excavations were carried out on the hill of Epano Englianos, southwest of Khora, at what has come to be known as the 'Palace of Nestor'. In addition to Blegen, those taking part included Bert Hodge Hill, W. McDonald and Mrs. Blegen. This brief excavation revealed remains of a Mycenaean palace complex with hundreds of Linear B tablets, the first to be discovered on the mainland, and fragments of frescoes. About one km south of the palace a tholos tomb, plundered in ancient times, was excavated. Fragments of gold and silver jewelry and of LH II, IIIA–B pottery were found (*AJA* 43, 1939, 557ff) (*ILN* June 3, 1939).

The excavations were finally resumed by Blegen in 1952. Kourouniotis had died in the interval and S. Marinatos represented the Greek Archaeological Service, though he largely concentrated on exploring other areas of Messenia. Excavation continued through 1966. Others taking part included Dr. and Mrs. Hill, Mrs. Blegen, W. McDonald, G. Mylonas, D. Theocharis, E. Vanderpool, M. Rawson, R. Hope, Lord William Taylour, Piet de Jong, Watson Smith, R. J. Buck, E. L. Bennett Jr., R. Hubbe, Mr. and Mrs. W. P. Donovan, M. Lang, G. Papathanasopoulos, D. French, Mr. and Mrs. W. G. Kittredge, Peter Smith and J. Pedley.

The site was occupied at least from the MH period to LH IIIB. The present palace complex was built in the LH IIIB period. The hill had been cleared and leveled for its construction, and there was probably an earlier palace. The hill had once been surrounded by a fortification wall, perhaps built in the LH I period, but there appear to have been no fortifications in the LH IIIB period, at least no evidence of any was found in the area of the excavation. A lower town occupied from MH–LHIIIB was partially excavated to the southwest, west and northwest of the palace. A chamber tomb cemetery was excavated about 300 m northwest of the palace. In addition to the tholos excavated in 1939, two others were excavated. One, to the northeast of the palace, excavated in 1953, had lined up with the gate of the fortification wall. It dates from transitional MH/LH I period and the latest burials probably antedated the construction of the LH IIIB palace. The other 'tholos' excavated in 1957 about 150 m from the palace, is probably rather a grave circle with burials, some in jars, some in pits. It dates from MH/LH I period and continued in use to LH III. Finds included pieces of boars' tusks and a Palace Style jar.

G. Papathanasopoulos investigated modern threshing floors in the vicinity of the palace attempting to locate more tholoi. Under one he found remains of a Mycenaean building, and under another the remains of two circular or apsidal houses, probably EH. Part of a proto-Geo-metric tholos tomb was excavated towards Koryphasion (q.v.). The town and palace were evidently destroyed toward the end of LH IIIB and were not reoccupied, though there is a little evidence of LH IIIC habitation in the region south of the palace (see Koryphasion). Preliminary reports are found in *AJA* (57, 1953, 59ff and in subsequent years through 1965), and final reports are as follows: *The Palace of Nestor I:* C. W. Blegen and Marion Rawson, *The Buildings and Their Contents,* Princeton 1966; *The Palace of Nestor II:* M. Lang, *The Frescoes,* Princeton 1968; *The Palace of Nestor III:* C. W. Blegen et al., *The Acropolis and Lower Town; Tholoi, Grave Circle, Chamber Tombs; Discoveries Outside the Citadel,* Princeton 1973 (cf. Desborough 94).

Other discoveries have been reported from the area of Khora. In the village S. Marinatos discovered prehistoric sherds, perhaps Neolithic, in the Katavothra cave (*AR* 1955, 16). On a hill west of the church of Ayios Ioannis to the southwest of the village Marinatos excavated two LH IIIB chamber tombs and noted others. He also uncovered a large Roman bath (*PAE* 1954, 305ff) (*AJA* 1969, no. 41 A) (*UMME* no. 21).

At 'Volimidia' about 800 m northeast of the village Marinatos exca-vated about 30 chamber tombs in a large cemetery between 1952 and 1954, in 1960 and in 1964–65. The chambers were generally round, cut from the rock in imitation of built tholoi. They date from LH I–IIIB. Traces of the settlement were noted 500 m away, with remains of walls, but little else. There was also a Hellenistic and Roman settlement and traces of Hellenistic and Roman cult have been found in some of the My-cenaean tombs. In 1964 an MH cist grave with numerous arrowheads, knives and other weapons was excavated (*PAE* 1952, 473ff; 1953, 238ff; 1954, 299ff; 1960, 198ff; 1964, 78ff; 1965, 102ff) (*Ergon* 1954, 41f; 1960, 146ff; 1964, 77ff; 1965, 76ff) (*BCH* 1953, 214ff; 1954, 120ff; 1955, 247ff; 1961, 703ff; 1965, 734ff).

**KOKLA (Triphylias):** On the Rakhi Khani hill on the north side of the village a large cemetery of Hellenistic and Roman cist graves was dis-covered. N. Yialouris conducted a rescue excavation in 1963 and dis-covered indications of a large EH, MH and LH habitation site (*AD* 19, 1964, *Chr.* 1, 154f) (*UMME* no. 224).

**KORONI (Pylias):** Modern Koroni is probably the site of ancient Messenian Asine, a settlement from Asine in Argos. For older bibliography and remains, see Frazer (Frazer, *Pausanias* 3, 449f) and M. N. Tod (*JHS* 25, 1905, 36f). It perhaps received its present name from a transfer of population from ancient Koroni, now Petalidi, in the Middle Ages. There are ancient fragments in the medieval fortress. M. N. Valmin excavated a Roman building with mosaics by the church of Ayia Triada (Valmin 1938, 469ff).

**KORYPHASION (Pylias):** In 1926 K. Kourouniotis and Ph. Stavropoulos excavated a tholos tomb about 800 m southwest of Koryphasion village (formerly Osman Aga, not the site of ancient Koryphasion), between Khora and Navarino Bay. It is one of the earliest tholoi yet known, dating from late MH and LH I (*PAE* 1925–26, 140ff) (cf. *Hesperia* 23, 1954, 158ff) (*UMME* no. 5).

Northeast of Koryphasion, at 'Mavroudia' about 3 km south of the Pylos palace, Lord William Taylour in 1958–59 excavated a Mycenaean chamber tomb. Finds were largely LH IIIB with some IIIC. A short distance to the west a proto-Geometric tholos, partly destroyed by the road, was excavated (*The Palace of Nestor III,* Princeton 1973, 224ff; 237ff) (*AJA* 1961, 238f) (*UMME* no. 2) (Desborough 94).

At 'Beyler Bey' about one km south of the village, S. Marinatos noted an LH IIIA–B habitation site (*PAE* 1960, 197) (*AJA* 1961, no. 56) (*UMME* no. 4), and another LH site was noted at 'Portes' southwest of the village, with some indications of Classical and Hellenistic occupation (*AJA* 1961, no. 55) (*UMME* no. 3).

**KOUKOUNARA (Pylias):** Between 1958 and 1961, and in 1963, S. Marinatos excavated a number of sites around Koukounara, about 15 km northeast of modern Pylos. At 'Katarrakhaki' in the gorge of the Arapi torrent about one km northeast of the village, a settlement was partially excavated dating from the LH I–LH IIIB periods. A number of tholoi were excavated. At 'Gouvoulari' near the settlement some of the tholoi dated from the LH I period. Another mound covered three small 'tholoi' chambers without dromoi, of late Mycenaean date. Other tholoi were found at 'Livaditi', 'Polla Dendra' and 'Akona', and to the south of Koukounara toward Stenosia at 'Londariti' and 'Phyties'. The latest burials were of LH IIIB date. Further southwest, toward Skhinolakka village at 'Palaiokhorafa', a burial mound and stone peribolos were excavated. The burials were all disturbed but appear to have been placed on the level floor and covered with slabs and earth. The finds were poor hand-made vases, perhaps of LH IIIC date. Nearby a complex of several rooms was excavated. LH IIIB pithoi and clay bathtubs were found (*PAE* 1960, 195ff; 1961, 174ff; 1963, 114ff) (*Ergon* 1958, 150ff; 1959, 117ff; 1960, 145f; 1961, 169ff; 1963, 81ff) (*AJA* 1961, 1969, nos. 65, 65 A) (*UMME* nos. 35, 36).

G. Korres resumed excavation in the cemeteries at Phyties and Gouvoulari in 1973–74. At Phyties an unplundered LH IIB/IIIA burial was found in a tholos. At Gouvoulari two tumuli complexes were excavated covering a number of small tholoi and U-shaped graves of LH I–IIIB date (*Ergon* 1974, 78ff) (*AR* 1974–75, 17).

**KYPARISSIA (Triphylias):** Modern Kyparissia occupies the site of the ancient city. For possible locations of places mentioned by Pausanias (IV 36.7) and earlier bibliography see Frazer (Frazer, *Pausanias* 3, 462f). N. Kyparissis conducted a trial excavation in 1911 and uncovered Roman remains at 'Mousga' and 'Phoros' possibly associated with the Roman forum (*PAE* 1911, 247ff). N. Yialouris excavated more Roman buildings here in 1961 and a Roman cemetery to the north (*AD* 17, 1961–62, *Chr.* 96ff). Further chance finds and rescue excavations have been reported, including Hellenistic houses (*AD* 23, 1968, *Chr.* 1, 157ff) and a Hellenistic cemetery and further Roman buildings (*AD* 26, 1971, *Chr.* 1, 124ff). M. N. Valmin had reported finding matt-painted and Mycenaean pottery (*Bull. Lund* 1928–29, 34f, 141; 1929–30, 1ff).

**LAMBAINA (Messinis):** At 'Tourkokivouro' about one km southeast of this village, G. Papathanasopoulos in a trial excavation in 1963 identified an EH, LH and Geometric site and excavated an empty slab grave, probably EH (*AD* 19, 1964, *Chr.* 1, 153f) (*AJA* 1964, 1969, no. 77 B) (*UMME* no. 122).

**LONGA (Pylias):** W. McDonald and N. Yialouris conducted a trial excavation in 1959 on the Kaphirio spur about 1.25 km southwest of Longa village, above the west coast of the Messinian gulf. Traces of a settlement were found, sherds of MH, LH IIIA–B, possibly sub-Mycenaean, and proto-Geometric. A possible tholos was noted under the Ayios Elias chapel, and Hellenistic and Roman buildings between Kaphirio and Longa (*AJA* 1961, no. 75) (*UMME* no. 107) (Desborough 95f).

**MALTHI (Triphylias):** The ancient site known as Malthi is situated on the northern end of a long spur to the west of Vasiliko village, in whose territory it lies. Malthi village (formerly Bodia) is a considerable distance to the southwest. In 1926 M. N. Valmin (M. N. Svensson) excavated two tholoi below this ridge on the west. Both these tombs, referred to in reports as the 'Bodia' tholoi, were plundered. Some LH IIIB material, and some perhaps LH IIIC was recovered. Valmin also noted the prehistoric settlement on the ridge above (*Bull. Lund* 1926–27, 53ff). Valmin excavated the settlement site briefly in 1929 and then in 1933–36. A walled town with a maze of houses, some apsidal, was uncovered. A number of MH cist or pit tombs of children were found within the settlement. Valmin placed the floruit of the town in the Mycenaean period and identified it with Homeric Dorion, but this has been questioned. The fortification wall and the most important period of the town were apparently MH. The Neolithic and EH remains noted by Valmin are doubtfully that early. Although the town continued in existence to the end of LH IIIB and possibly into LH IIIC, a number of other important Mycenaean settlements are now known in the vicinity which could as easily be equated with Dorion (M. N. Valmin, *The Swedish Messenia Expedition,* Lund 1938) (*AJA* 1961, 1969, no. 27; 1969, 141 notes) (*UMME* no. 222) (Desborough 94).

To the west of the Malthi site at 'Gouves' is another Mycenaean complex, discovered by Valmin in 1936. He returned to this site in 1952 and excavated a number of rooms. Some Mycenaean stone reliefs were found (*Op. Ath.* 1, 1953, 29ff; 2, 1955, 66ff). This 'lower town' area is very large and only a very small portion has been excavated. It was perhaps more important than Malthi itself in the LH IIIB period, Malthi perhaps being a citadel for refuge in insecure times. Further excavations were carried out in 1960 (*AD* 16, 1960, *Chr.* 119ff) (*AJA* 1969, 27 A) (*UMME* no. 223).

**MESSENE:** The city of Messene lay in the hollow southwest of the steep acropolis of Ithomi, around the modern town of Mavromati. At least from Archaic times Ithomi was a religious center and rallying point for Messenian rebellions, but the site was apparently not inhabited until it became an administrative center in the Hellenistic period. Th. Sophoulis in 1895 excavated a fountain which was probably the Arsinoë fountain in the agora (*PAE* 1895, 27). For early bibliography and description, see Frazer (Frazer, *Pausanias* 3, 429ff). In 1909 the stadium and Hellenistic houses were explored by G. Oikonomos (*PAE* 1909, 201ff). He again excavated in 1925, uncovering a public building, probably the Synedrion or Council house, and a heroon with four tombs and an altar (*PAE* 1925, 55ff). A. Orlandos resumed excavations for the Archaeological Society in 1957. He continued work through 1964 and again from 1969 to the present, excavating Hellenistic and later buildings around the agora (*PAE* for years 1957 through 1960, 1962 through 1964; 1969 to present) (*Ergon* for years 1969 through 1974).

**METHONI (Pylias):** M. N. Valmin explored the area of Methoni and noted Archaic to Medieval remains on the site of Methoni castle (Valmin 1930, 152ff). G. Papathanasopoulos observed part of a probably Roman fortification wall during repairs to the medieval fortress in 1961 (*AD* 17, 1961–62, *Chr.* 94; 18, 1963, *Chr.* 1, 92ff).

On the Nisakouli islet on the southeast side of Methoni Bay A. Khoremis conducted a trial excavation in 1968, uncovering what is probably an MH altar with remains of two walls, animal bones and sherds. A pithos burial and a simple earth burial were excavated, and walls of a building. Black and grey Minyan and matt-painted wares were found. The site was much denuded. It was perhaps joined to the mainland in the prehistoric period (*AAA* 2, 1969, 10ff) (*AJA* 1969, no. 72D) (*UMME* no. 80).

**MOURIATADA (Triphylias):** In 1960 S. Marinatos excavated a Mycenaean settlement on the Elleniko spur about one km east of this village east of Kyparissia. There is a fine Cyclopean fortification wall, a large megaron with fragments of painted plaster, and another megaron-type building which Marinatos suggested might be a temple. The settlement perhaps lasted into the LH IIIC period. A plundered tholos was excavated nearby (*PAE* 1960, 201ff) (*Ergon* 1960, 149ff) (*AD* 16, 1960, *Chr.* 116f) (*AJA* 1969, no. 22 A) (*UMME* no. 201) (Desborough 93f).

**MYRON (Triphylias):** Between 1960 and 1965 S. Marinatos excavated an early Mycenaean settlement on the Perivolia hill about one km north of Myron, 9 km northeast of Kyparissia. The settlement covered the whole hilltop, which was protected by a Cyclopean wall on the one accessible side. Two large tholoi were excavated. From tholos 1, apparently plundered during Mycenaean times, came fragments of LH I–III pottery and embossed gold sheeting. On the door jamb a branch and a double axe were engraved. A layer of what is probably debris from Classical and Hellenistic sacrifices was found. Tholos 2 was also plundered. A house of transitional MH/LH I period had been destroyed when the tholos was built. Cist graves of children were found beneath the house floor. Next to tholos 2 a small third tholos was discovered. It had been plundered, but a central trench was still intact. Rich gold offerings including cups, a diadem and dress ornaments were found. Tholoi 2 and 3 were partially surrounded by a semicircular wall. Five hundred meters to the west of the site an MH tumulus with pithos burials was excavated in 1964 (*PAE* for years 1960 through 1965) (*Ergon* for years 1960 through 1965) (*ILN* Dec. 4, 1965, 32f) (*AD* 21, 1966, *Chr.* 1, 166ff).

**MYRSINOKHORI (Pylias):** In 1956 and 1957 S. Marinatos excavated two tholos tombs on the Routsi ridge by Myrsinokhori, east of Epano Englianos. One was unplundered. The earliest burials were in two slab-covered pits in the floor. One contained four or five burials, two inlaid daggers, other weapons, a silver cup, mirrors and gems. The second pit contained the burial of a young girl. The latest burial was on the floor of the chamber; swords, daggers and a number of gems were found with it. The vases from the tholos date from LH IIA–IIIA. A number may be Minoan imports. A smaller plundered tholos was also excavated. LH III vases were found. There was a hearth at the entrance to the dromos (*PAE* 1956, 203ff; 1957, 118ff) (*Ergon* 1956, 91ff; 1957, 70ff) (*ILN* April 6, 1957, 540ff) (*AJA* 1961, no. 48) (*UMME* no. 54).

At 'Vaies' about 2 km to the west G. Papathanasopoulos conducted a trial excavation on what is a small LH site. It is about one km east of the palace at Epano Englianos, but is separated from it by a steep ravine (*AD* 19, 1964, *Chr.* 1, 150f) (*AJA* 1969, no. 42 B) (*UMME* no. 55).

**PAPPOULIA (Pylias):** About one km west of Pappoulia at 'Ayios Ioannis' S. Marinatos excavated in 1954 and 1955 a probably early MH burial mound. In the middle of the mound was an empty U-shaped chamber.

Pithoi, each containing one or two contracted burials, had been inserted at intervals into the outside of the mound. At the village, Marinatos excavated four small and badly destroyed LH III tholoi (*PAE* 1954, 311ff; 1955, 254f) (*Ergon* 1954, 42-43; 1955, 91) (*AJA* 1961, no. 50) (*UMME* no. 52).

**PETALIDI (Pylias):** Modern Petalidi on the Messenian gulf is the site of ancient Koroni. For earlier bibliography and description see Frazer (Frazer, *Pausanias* 3, 447), M. N. Tod (*JHS* 25, 1905, 40), and C. A. Roebuck (Roebuck 18ff). There are remains of Classical and Hellenistic fortifications on the acropolis above the village. Inscriptions and Hellenistic and Roman statues have been found (*BSA* 1957, 249ff; 1966, 124) (*AR* 1959, 12; 1960, 11).

**PHOINIKOUS (Pylias):** West of Phoinikous (formerly Taverna) on the Ayia Analipsis hill are the remains of a fairly large prehistoric site, where EH, MH and LH IIIA–B and possibly LH I–II material has been noted. There are also Geometric and later remains. The hill has been eroded by the sea. It was investigated by M. N. Valmin (Valmin 1930, 155ff). There is a Roman site to the west (*BCH* 1959, 641). There are also possibly the remains of a burial mound and a tholos in the vicinity to the east (*AJA* 1961, no. 73) (*UMME* no. 79).

**PLATANOVRYSIS (Pylias):** A. Khoremis examined a small tholos tomb at 'Genitsari' near Platanovrysis, south of Khandrinos. It was completely empty but some LH sherds were found outside (*AD* 23, 1968, *Chr.* 1, 156; 24, 1969, *Chr.* 1, 145).

**PROTI ISLAND:** M. N. Valmin explored a late Classical or Hellenistic fortress on the island, the ancient Prokonnesos (*Bull. Lund* 1928–29, 45ff) (Valmin 1930, 141ff).

**PYLA (Pylias):** An Archaic pithos burial was reported by P. Themelis near Pyla, northeast of modern Pylos. The pithos also contained iron swords and bronze vases (*AD* 20, 1965, *Chr.* 2, 208).

**PYLOS:** The following description includes sites around Navarino Bay. For 'the Palace of Nestor' see Khora. For a good early description of the area of the bay and early bibliography see Frazer (Frazer, *Pausanias* 3, 456ff).

On the north side of the bay is the Osman Aga or Divari lagoon, now partly drained. It is cut off from the bay by a sand bar, and from the sea by the rocky promontory with the medieval Palaiokastro fortress which marks the north end of Navarino bay. To the north of Palaiokastro is the very small Voïdokoilia harbour which is separated from the lagoon by sandbanks.

Palaiokastro is the Medieval Navarino, the site of Classical Koryphasion, the Pylos of Thucydides. (For Medieval remains see *JHS* 16, 1896, 1ff.) In the north face of the acropolis is the so-called Cave of Nestor. H. Schliemann visited the site in 1874 and 1888. He made some soundings in the acropolis but found nothing ancient. He reported 'Mycenaean' type ware from the cave (*AM* 14, 1889, 132ff). In 1896 a French expedition briefly explored the cave and recovered ware later recognized as 'matt-painted' (*BCH* 1896, 388ff). In 1953 W. McDonald and D. Theocharis dug a trial trench in the cave. There is evidence of Neolithic inhabitation and use in EH, MH, LH III and Classical periods (*AJA* 1964, no. 32) (*UMME* no. 10). In 1958 S. Marinatos investigated within the area of ancient Koryphasion. Below the fortress on the north side he found LH IIIA–B sherds, traces of Archaic and Classical occupation, and parts of Hellenistic fortifications and houses (*Ergon* 1958, 148ff) (*AJA* 1961, no. 61) (*UMME* no. 9).

On the north side of Voïdokoilia Bay in 1956 Marinatos excavated a tholos tomb. It had been plundered, but two burials were found with arrowheads, beads and gold ornaments (*Ergon* 1956, 90ff) (*AJA* 1961, no. 60) (*UMME* no. 8). To the north of the bay an EH habitation site, perhaps also Neolithic and MH was noted (*AJA* 1961, no. 59) (*UMME* no. 6). Voïdokoilia Bay was perhaps the harbour of Mycenaean Pylos. The Osman Aga lagoon has also been discussed (W. K. Pritchett, *Studies in Ancient Greek Topography* 1, 1965, 6ff) (*UMME* 44ff; 240f) (*AJA* 1964, 1969 no. 59 A-E). The lagoon may have served as a harbour, but its extent and depth have varied, and it would have been necessary to keep a channel open through the sandbank. The north part was apparently above water at times as EH, MH, LH IIIB and proto-Geometric sherds have been found in the lagoon, also some Hellenistic and Roman material, but some of this may have been washed down by streams.

In 1964 and 1965 N. Yialouris excavated in an extensive Hellenistic cemetery between Yialova hamlet and Palaiokastro, mostly on the sand spit separating the bay and lagoon. Fifty-five cist graves were excavated. They were in groups surrounded by enclosures containing pyres (*AAA* 1, 1968, 189ff) (*AD* 20, 1965, *Chr.* 2, 208; 21, 1966, *Chr.* 1, 164ff).

Overlooking Navarino Bay, about 700 m southwest of the junction of the roads from Kalamata and Kyparissia, an LH III settlement was noted on the Vigla hill. It has partly fallen into the bay. Two probable tholos tombs were noted northeast of the road junction and Neolithic celts have been reported from the vicinity (*AJA* 1961, no. 63) (*UMME* no. 44) (*AJA* 43, 1939, 559).

Modern Pylos, or Neokastro or Navarino, does not seem to have been occupied in antiquity. The castle was built in the 16th century to replace the older castle (Palaiokastro) on the other side of the bay. The town dates chiefly from the 19th century.

**SAPIENTZA ISLAND:** In 1963 a shipwreck was examined off the north point of the island. The cargo was red granite columns. Another wreck was found to the north of it. Three sacrophagi, some amphora fragments, and a glass bottle date it to the 3rd century A.D. (*AD* 19, 1964, *Chr.* 1, 153).

**SKHIZA ISLAND:** In 1952 M. N. Valmin explored a cave on this island. Some MH, or perhaps Middle Minoan, pottery was found. It was probably a cult spot (*Op. Ath.* 1, 1953, 44ff) (*AJA* 1961, 254).

The other Oinoussai islands were occupied, though probably sparsely, in Roman times. They have been explored by Valmin, and by W. McDonald and R. Hope Simpson (Valmin 1930, 159ff) (*AJA* 1961, 254).

**SOULINARI (Pylias):** At 'Tourliditsa' about 2.5 km northwest of Soulinari, S. Marinatos excavated a small tholos tomb. Finds were from LH IIB–IIIA (*PAE* 1966, 129ff) (*Ergon* 1966, 107ff) (*AJA* 1969, no. 68 A) (*UMME* no. 29).

**THALAMAI (Kalamon):** The town of Thalamai and the oracle of Ino-

Pasiphae mentioned by Pausanias (III 26.1) are near the modern Koutiphari (renamed Thalamai) above the east coast of the Messenian gulf. The British School under G. Dickens excavated a Hellenistic spring house at 'Svina' to the east of the village, probably part of the oracle. An inscription with a dedication to Pasiphae had previously been found nearby (*BSA* 10, 1903–4, 161, 174; 11, 1904–5, 124ff). Some LH III sherds and an LH jar were found in this excavation (*BSA* 1957, 232f). Other antiquities including a 7th century head have been reported (*AD* 16, 1960, *Chr.* 107-8).

**TRAGANA (Triphylias):** In 1909 A. Skias investigated briefly a Mycenaean tholos tomb about 700 m southwest of this village northwest of modern Koryphasion (*PAE* 1909, 274ff). In 1912 K. Kourouniotis excavated the chamber but not the dromos. The tholos dates from the LH I/IIA period. It was used until the LH IIIA1 period, and after a gap, again used beginning in LH IIIC for burials in two rectangular pits in the floor. In the disturbed fill some further LH IIIC and some proto-Geometric vases were found. It is one of the very few clear instances of LH IIIC in the Pylos area. It was reused as a Hellenistic dwelling (*AE* 1914, 99ff). S. Marinatos re-examined it in 1955 and excavated the dromos. Two piles of bronze implements were found in the dromos. Marinatos also excavated a second tholos, also plundered, but one grave pit was found intact. It contained the remains of two cremated girls, perhaps the earliest case of Mycenaean cremation, dated by Marinatos to about 1400 B.C. Necklaces, a mirror and sealstones were found (*PAE* 1955, 247ff) (*Ergon* 1955, 88ff) (*AJA* 1961, no. 46) (*UMME* no. 11) (Desborough 95). At 'Voroulia' Marinatos excavated a small building with evidence of MH and LH I–II habitation. A large number of ritual vases and triton shells were recovered (*Ergon* 1956, 90) (*AJA* 1961, no. 45) (*UMME* no. 12).

Hellenistic tombs have been excavated by N. Yialouris and G. Papathanasopoulos. At 'Tsopani Rakhi' a low tumulus contained three slab-lined cist graves and two graves which had contained wooden coffins (*AD* 17, 1961–62, *Chr.* 98; 18, 1963, *Chr.* 1, 91f).

**VASILIKO (Triphylias):** At 'Xerovrysi' 1.5 km southeast of the village, just north of the railroad line, M. N. Valmin in 1927 excavated a tholos tomb. It had a small side chamber. The tomb was in use in the LH I–II periods and there was a cult in Classical and Hellenistic times (*Bull. Lund* 1926–27, 88f; 1927–28, 20ff) (*AJA* 1961, no. 28) (*UMME* no. 220).

**VLAKHOPOULO (Pylias):** On the Agrilia hill about 2.5 km northeast of the village, an LH settlement, possibly also MH, was noted. West of the hill a small tholos opened by villagers was examined by N. Yialouris and excavated by S. Marinatos. The finds, including knives and vases, are of the LH IIIA–B period (*PAE* 1964, 89ff) (*Ergon* 1964, 84f) (*AJA* 1969, no. 69 B) (*UMME* no. 25).

**VOUNARIA (Pylias):** At Vounaria on the west coast of the Messenian gulf north of Koroni, Classical and later inscriptions and tombs have been noted by M. N. Tod (*JHS* 25, 1905, 37ff) and M. N. Valmin (Valmin 1930, 171ff). A Classical and Hellenistic cemetery was found in 1960 (*AR* 1960, 11).

## References - Periodicals

| | |
|---|---|
| *AA* | *Archäologischer Anzeiger: Beiblatt zum Jahrbuch des Deutschen archäologischen Instituts* |
| *AAA* | *Athens Annals of Archaeology* |
| *AD* | *Archaiologikon Deltion* |
| *AE* | *Archaiologike Ephemeris* |
| *AJA* | *American Journal of Archaeology* |
| *AM* | *Mitteilungen des deutschen archäologischen Instituts; athenische Abteilung* |
| *Ann.* | *Annuario della Scuola Archeologica di Atene* |
| | *Antiquity* |
| | *Archaeologia* |
| *AR* | *Archaeological Reports* |
| | *Archaeology* |
| | *Art and Archaeology* |
| | *Athenaion* |
| *AZ* | *Archäologische Zeitung* |
| *BCH* | *Bulletin de Correspondance Hellénique* |
| *BSA* | *Annual of the British School at Athens* |
| *Bull. Lund* | *Bulletin de la Société Royale des Lettres de Lund* |
| | *Bulletin de l'école française d'Athènes* |
| | *Bulletino dell'Instituto di Corrisp. Archeol.* |
| | *Ellenika* |
| *Ergon* | *To Ergon tes Archaeologikes Etaireias kata to etos...* |
| | *Gazette Archéologique* |
| | *Gnomon* |
| *Hesperia* | *Hesperia, Journal of the American School of Classical Studies at Athens* |
| *ILN* | *Illustrated London News* |
| *Jahrbuch* | *Jahrbuch des deutschen archäologischen Instituts* |
| *JHS* | *Journal of Hellenic Studies* |
| *JÖAI* | *Jahreshefte des österreichischen archäologischen Instituts in Wien* |
| | *Journal of the Geographical Society* |
| | *Kathimerini* |
| | *Klio* |
| | *Liverpool Annals of Archaeology and Anthropology* |
| | *Metropolitan Museum Studies* |
| | *Mikra Meletimata* |
| | *Mnemosyne* |
| | *Neon Athinaion* |
| | *Neue Jahrbücher für Antike und deutsche Bildung* |
| *Op. Ath.* | *Opuscula Atheniensia* |
| *PAE* | *Praktika tes Archaiologikes Etaireias* |
| | *Papers of the American School at Athens* |
| | *Parnassos* |
| | *Phoenix* |

*Pictorial*
*Polemon*
*Praktika tis Akadimias Athinon*
*Science Journal*
*Zeitschrift für Altertumswissenschaft*

**References - Books**

*L'Acropole d'Athènes*, I-II, E. Beulé. Paris 1953–54.

AGC 3    *Ancient Greek Cities no. 3: Corinthia-Cleonaea*, M. Sakellariou and N. Faraklas. Athens Technological Organization, Athens Center of Ekistics, Athens 1971.

AGC 8    *Ancient Greek Cities no. 8: Sikyonia*, N. Faraklas. Athens 1971.

AGC 10   *Ancient Greek Cities no. 10: Troizinia, Kalaureia, Methana*. Athens 1971.

AGC 11   *Ancient Greek Cities no. 11: Phleiasia*, N. Faraklas. Athens 1972.

AGC 12   *Ancient Greek Cities no. 12: Epidauria*, N. Faraklas. Athens 1972.

AGC 14   *Ancient Greek Cities no. 14: Megaris, Aigosthena, Ereneia*, M. Sakellariou and N. Pharaklas. Athens 1972.

AGC 17   *Ancient Greek Cities no. 17: Athens, Ekistic Elements, First Report*, J. Travlos. Athens 1972.

AGC 19   *Ancient Greek Cities no. 19: Hermionis-Halias*, N. Faraklas. Athens 1973.

AGC 21   *Ancient Greek Cities no. 21: Attica, Ekistic Elements, First Report*, M. Petropoulakou and E. Pentazos. Athens 1973.

AGC 23   *Ancient Greek Cities no. 23: Megale Polis in Arkadia*, A. Petronatis. Athens 1973.

*Aghios Kosmas*, G. E. Mylonas. Princeton 1959.

Agora XIII   *Agora XIII, The Neolithic and Bronze Ages*, S. A. Immerwahr. 1971.

Agora XIV    *Agora XIV, The Agora of Athens; the History, Shape and Uses of an Ancient City Center*, H.A. Thompson and R.E. Wycherly. Princeton 1972.

Alt-Athen    *Alt-Athen und seine Agora*, vol. 1, W. Dörpfeld. 1937.

*Alt-Olympia*, 2 vols., W. Dörpfeld. Berlin 1935.

*Anastilosis tis stoas tis Brauronos*, Kh. Boura, Dimosieumata tou Arkhaiologikou Deltiou XI. Athens 1967.

*Ancient Corinth: A Guide to the Excavations*, 6th ed., rev., J.L. Caskey. 1960.

*Ancient Landscapes, Studies in Field Archaeology*, J. Bradford. London 1957.

*Ancient Mycenae*, G. E. Mylonas. 1957.

*Ancient Sikyon*, C. H. Skalet. Baltimore 1928.

*The Antiquities of Athens*, 4 vols. J. Stuart and N. Revett. London 1762–1816.

*Der Apollotempel zu Bassae in Arcadia und die daselbst ausgegrabenen Bildwerke,* von Stackelberg. Frankfurt am Main 1826.

*Archaeologische Studien,* C. Blinkenberg. Copenhagen 1904.

*The Archaic Cemetery,* Scheibler, Kerameikos Book no. 3. Athens 1973.

*Archäologische Aufsätze,* 2 vols., L. Ross. Leipzig 1855–1861.

*The Argive Heraion,* 2 vols., C. Waldstein et al. Boston 1902.

*Argolis,* H. Lehmann. Deutches archäologisches Institut. Athens 1937.

*Argos and the Argolid,* R. A. Tomlinson. London 1972.

*Argos, les fouilles de la Deiras, Études péloponnésiennes IV,* J. Deshayes. Paris 1966.

*Arkadiki Alipheira kai ta Mnimeia tis,* A. K. Orlandos. Library of the Athenian Archaeological Society no. 58, 1967–68.

*Arkadische Forschungen,* F. Hiller von Gärtringen and H. Latterman. Berlin 1911.

*Asine: Results of the Swedish Excavations 1922–1930,* A. W. Persson. Stockholm 1938.

*Athènes de Tibère à Trajan,* Paul Graindor. Cairo 1930.

*Athènes sous Auguste,* Paul Graindor. Cairo 1927.

*Athènes sous Hadrien,* Paul Graindor. Cairo 1934.

*The Athenian Agora: A Guide to the Excavations and Museum,* 2nd ed. Athens 1962.

*The Athens Agora. Results of Excavations Conducted by the American School of Classical Studies at Athens,* vols. I to XX (not published in order). Princeton 1953–74.

*Die Ausgrabung der Akropolis vom Jahre 1885 bis zum Jahre 1890,* P. Cavvadias and G. Kawerau. Athens 1906.

*Ausgrabungen um Panathenäischen Stadion,* E. Ziller. Berlin 1870.

*Berichte über die Ausgrabungen in Olympia,* 8 vols. German Institute, Berlin 1837–.

*Bericht über die Untersuchungen auf der Akropolis von Athen in Frühjahre 1862,* C. Bötticher. Berlin 1863.

*Brauron: Guide to the Site and Museum,* P. G. Themelis. Athens 1971.

*The Catalogue of Ships in Homer's Iliad,* J. F. Lazenby. Oxford 1970.

*Catalogue of the Sparta Museum,* M.N. Tod and A.J.B. Wace. Oxford 1906.

*The Chronology of Mycenaean Pottery,* A. Furumark. 1941.

*Corinth,* vols. I through XVI. Harvard University Press, Cambridge, Mass. 1932–64.

*Crete and Mycenae,* S. Marinatos and M. Hirmer. 1960.

*Das Dionysos-Theater in Athen I–III.* E. Fiechter. Stuttgart 1935–36.

Desborough *The Last Mycenaeans and Their Successors,* V.R. d'A. Desborough. Oxford 1964.

Dodwell   *A Classical and Topographical Tour through Greece,* 2 vols., E. Dodwell.
Tour      London 1819.

           *Eleusis and the Eleusinian Mysteries,* G.E. Mylonas. Princeton 1961.

Eliot      *Coastal Demes of Attica,* C.W.J. Eliot. *Phoenix* Suppl. V, Toronto 1962.

*Enciclopedia dell' arte antica classica e orientale.* Rome 1964.

*The Erechtheum,* L.D. Caskey et al. Cambridge, Mass. 1927.

*L'Établissement thermal de Gortys d'Arcadie, Études Peloponnésiennes II.* R. Ginouvès, l'École française d'Athènes. Paris 1959.

*Excavation in the Barbouna Area at Asine,* R. and I. Hägg, ed. Uppsala 1973.

*The Excavation of the Athenian Acropolis 1882–90,* J.A. Bundgaard. Copenhagen 1974.

*Excavations at Berbati,* G. Säflund. Stockholm 1965.

*Excavations at Megalopolis 1890–91,* E. Gardner et al., *JHS* Suppl. no. 1, 1892.

*Excavations of the American School of Athens at the Heraion of Argos I,* C. Waldstein. London 1892.

*Expédition scientifique de Morée,* A. Blouet et al. Paris 1831.

*La Forteresse de Rhamnonte,* J. Pouilloux. Paris 1954.

*Fouilles de Épidaure I,* P. Kavvadias. Athens 1893.

*Fouilles de Lycosoura,* P. Kavvadias. Athens 1893.

Frazer,  *Pausanias's Description of Greece,* volume II, J. G. Frazer. London
Pausanias  1898.

Gazetteer  *A Gazetteer and Atlas of Mycenaean Sites,* R. Hope Simpson, Institute of Classical Studies, University of London, Suppl. no. 16, 1965.

*Die Gräber der Argolis I, Uppsala Studies in Ancient Mediterranean and Near Eastern Civilization,* Robin Hägg. Uppsala 1974.

*Grave Circle B of Mycenae, Studies in Mediterranean Archaeology no. 7,* G.E. Mylonas. Lund 1964.

*Greek Fortifications,* F.E. Winter. Univ. of Toronto Press 1971.

*The Greek Temple Builders at Epidauros,* A. Burford. Liverpool 1969.

*Greek Walls,* R.L. Scranton. Harvard University Press 1941.

*Das griechische Theater,* W. Dörpfeld and E. Reisch. Athens 1896.

*Guide to Mycenae,* 4th ed., A.J.B. Wace and Williams. 1966.

Hesperia  *Fortified Military Camps in Attica,* James R. McCredie. *Hesperia*
Suppl.XI  Suppl. XI, 1966.

Hill  *The Ancient City of Athens,* I.T. Hill. London 1953.

*Hira und Andania, Einundsiebzigstes Programm sum Winckelmannsfeste,* H. von Gärtringen and H. Latterman. Berlin 1911.

*The History and Civilization of Ancient Megara,* Johns Hopkins Univ. Studies in Archaeology no. 2, E.L. Highbarger. Baltimore 1927.

*100 Jahre deutsche Ausgrabung in Olympia,* Austellung veranstaltet vom Organisationskomitee für die Spide des XX. Olympiade. Munich 1972.

*Ieron tou Asklipiou en Epidauro,* P. Kavvadias. Athens 1900.

IG  *Inscriptiones Graecae,* 15 vols. De Gruyter, 1873–1939.

*Isthmia,* 2 vols., O. Broneer. American School of Classical Studies at Athens, Princeton 1971–73.

*Istoria tis Poleos Aigiou apo ton mythikon Khronon Mekhri ton Imeron Mas,* A. Stavropoulou. Patrai 1954.

*Istoria tis Poleos Patron apo Arkhaiotaton Khronon Mekhri 1821,* S. N. Thomopoulou. Patrai 1950.

Judeich        *Topographie von Athen*, 2nd ed., W. Judeich. Munich 1931.
               *Katalogs tou Mouseiou Lykosouras*, K. Kourouniotis. Athens 1911.
               *Kerameikos, Ergebnisse des Ausgrabungen*, 6 vols. to date, Deutsches
                  archäologisches Institut. Berlin 1939–70.
               *Korakou*, C. W. Blegen. American School of Classical Studies at
                  Athens 1921.
               *Das Kuppelgrab bei Menidi*, H.G. Lolling et al., Deutsches Archaeolog-
                  isches Institut. Athens 1880.
               *Lerna I, The Fauna*, N.-G. Gejvall. Princeton 1969.
               *Lerna II, The People*, J. L. Angel. Princeton 1971.
               *Mantinée et l'Arcadie orientale*, G. Fougères. Paris 1898.
               *Metallurgy in Antiquity*, R. J. Forbes. Leiden 1950.
Meyer 1939     *Peloponnesische Wanderungen*, Ernst Meyer. Leipzig and Zürich 1939.
Meyer 1957     *Neue Peloponnesische Wanderungen*, Ernst Meyer. Bern 1957.
               *Mikinaiki Akropolis ton Athinon*, S. Iakovidis. Athens 1962.
               *Mikra Meletimata*, K. A. Romaios. Thessaloniki 1958.
Milchhöfer     *Erlaüternder Text zu den Karten von Attika*, A. Milchhöfer et al. Berlin
                  1881–1900.
               *Un milliardaire antique, Hérode Atticus et sa famille*, Paul Graindor.
                  Cairo 1930.
               *Les Mines du Laurion*, E. Ardaillon. 1897.
               *The Minoan-Mycenaean Religion and Its Survival in Greek Religion*, 2nd
                  ed., Martin P. Nilsson. Lund 1950.
               *Les Monuments de l'Acropole, relevement et conservation*, N. Balanos.
                  Paris 1939.
               *The Mycenaean Age*, Kh. Tsountas. London 1897.
               *Mycenae: A Narrative of Researches and Discoveries at Mycenae and
                  Tiryns*, H. Schliemann. New York 1880.
               *Mycenae and the Mycenaean Age*, G. E. Mylonas. Princeton 1966.
               *Mycenaean Pottery*, A. Furumark. 1941.
               *The Mycenaeans*, Wm. Taylour. New York 1964.
               *Mykinai kai Mykinaios Politismos*, Kh. Tsountas. Athens 1893.
               *Mythology and Monuments of Ancient Athens*, J. E. Harrison and M.
                  de G. Verral. London 1890.
               *New Tombs at Dendra near Midea*, A. W. Persson. Lund 1942.
               *Olympia, die Ergebnisse der vom deutschen Reich veranstalteten Aus-
                  grabungen*, 5 vols., E. Curtius and F. Adler. Berlin 1890–97.
               *Olympia*, H.-V. Hermann. Munich 1972.
               *Olympia*, Alfred Mallwitz. Munich 1972.
               *Olympia, Its History and Remains*, E.N. Gardiner. Washington D.C.
                  1925, repr. 1971.
               *Olympische Forschungen*, E. Kunze and H. Schlief, eds.; 7 vols. Ber-
                  lin 1944–.
               *Oropos kai to ieron tou Amphiaraou*, B. Petrakos. Athens 1968.
               *Ostraka ek Dekeleias*, Princesses Sophia and Eirene of Greece and
                  Th. A. Arvanitopoulos. Athens 1959.
               *The Palace of Nestor at Pylos in Western Messenia*, 3 vols., C. W. Blegen
                  and M. Rawson. Princeton 1966–73.

*Panathenaic Prize Amphoras,* J. Frel, Kerameikos Book 2. Athens 1973.

Papado-   *The Archaeology of Mycenaean Achaea,* A. J. Papadopoulos. Univ. of
poulos     London Ph.D. Thesis 1972.

Perachora   *The Sanctuaries of Hera Arkaia and Limenia, Perachora I and II,* H. Payne
et al. Oxford 1940–62.

*Le Pirée,* Ch. Th. Panagos. Athens 1968.

*The Pompeion,* W. Hoepfner, Kerameikos Book 1. Athens 1971.

*Primitive Athens as Described by Thucydides,* J. E. Harrison, Cambridge 1906.

*Proistoria tis Peloponnisou,* K. Syriopoulos. Athens 1964.

*Proistorikai Athenai,* M. A. Pantelidou. Athens 1975.

*Proistoriki Eleusis,* G. E. Mylonas. Athens 1932.

*Prosymna: The Helladic Settlement Preceding the Argive Heraion,* C. W.
Blegen. Cambridge 1937.

RE     *Realencyclopädie der classischen Altertumswissenschaft,* Pauly-
Wissowa.

Roebuck   *A History of Messenia,* C. A. Roebuck. Chicago 1941.

*The Royal Tombs at Dendra near Midea,* A. W. Persson. Lund 1931.

*Le Sanctuaire d'Aléa Athéna,* C. Dugas et al. Paris 1924.

*Le Sanctuaire d'Apollon pythéen d'Argos, Études péloponnésiennes* I,
C. W. Vollgraff. École française d'Athènes. Paris 1956.

*The Sanctuary of Artemis Orthia at Sparta,* R. M. Dawkins et al. *JHS*
Suppl. no. 5. London 1929.

*A Sanctuary of Zeus on Mt. Hymetta,* M. K. Langdon. *Hesperia* Suppl.
XVI 1976.

*Die Schachtgräber von Mykenai,* G. Karo. 1930.

*Schliemann's Excavations,* C. Schuchhardt. London 1891.

Scoufo-   *Mycenaean Citadels,* N. C. Scoufopoulos, *Studies in Mediterranean
poulos     Archaeology* no. 22. Göteborg 1971.

*Sounion,* 2nd. ed., W. B. Dinsmoor, Jr. Athens 1974.

*Studies in Ancient Greek Topography,* W. K. Pritchett. Berkeley, Calif.
1969.

*Studies in Ancient Technology,* vols. 7–9. R. J. Forbes. N.Y. 1971–72.

*Submycenaean Studies,* C.-G. Styrenius. Lund 1967.

*The Swedish Excavations at Asea in Arcadia,* E. J. Holmberg. Göteborg 1944.

*Symbole stin melete tou ergou tou Agorakritou,* G. Despinis. Athens
1971.

*Taphikos Kyklos B tou Mykinou,* 2 vols., G. E. Mylonas. Athens 1972.

*The Technique of Early Greek Sculpture,* S. Casson, repr. of 1933 ed.,
Hacher Art Books, New York 1970.

*Der Tempel der Nike Apteros,* L. Ross, E. Schaubert, Chr. Hansen.
Berlin 1839.

*The Temple of Zeus at Nemea,* B. H. Hill, rev. and suppl. by L. K. Williams, Am. School Classical Studies at Athens. Princeton 1966.

*The Theater at Isthmia,* E. R. Gebbard. Chicago 1973.

*Das Theater in Oropos, Antike Griechische Theaterbauten,* Heft 1, E.
Fiechter. Stuttgart 1930.

*Das Theater in Sikyon*, E. Fiechter. Stuttgart 1931.

*Das Theater von Epidauros*, A. von Gerkau and W. Müller-Wiener. Paris 1961.

*Ta Theatra tou Peiraios kai o kophos limin*, I. Ch. Dragatsis. Athens 1882.

*The Theatre of Dionysos in Athens*, A. W. Pickard-Cambridge. Oxford 1946.

*Le théâtron à gradins droits et l'odéon, Études péloponnésiennes VI*, R. Ginouvès. Paris 1972.

*Thorikos: A Guide to the Excavations*, H. F. Mussche, Comité des Fouilles Belges en Grèce. Brussels 1974.

*Thorikos and the Laurion in Archaic and Classical Times, Colloquy March 1973, Miscellanea Graeca* I, H.F. Mussche, ed. State Univ. of Ghent 1974.

*Tiryns: The Prehistoric Palace of the Kings of Tiryns*, H. Schliemann. Repr. of 1885 ed. New York 1968.

*Tiryns VI*, K. Gebauer. Mainz 1974.

*Tombes géometriques d'Argos I (1952–1958), Études péloponnésiennes* VIII, P. Courbin. Paris 1956.

*The Topography of Athens*, W. M. Leake. London 1841.

*Travels in Asia Minor and Greece*, rev. ed., R. Chandler. 1825.

Travlos Dictionary     *Pictorial Dictionary of Ancient Athens*. J. Travlos. London 1971.

Travlos, Poleodomiki Exelikis     *Poleodomiki Exelixis ton Athinon*, J. Travlos. Athens 1960.

Trianta-phyllou     *Istorikon Lexikon ton Batron*, K. N. Triantaphyllou. Patrai 1959.

*Troizen und Kalaureia*, G. Welter. Berlin 1911.

*The Two Agoras in Ancient Athens*, A. N. Oikonomides. Chicago 1964.

UMME     *The Minnesota Messenia Expedition*, W. McDonald and G. R. Rapp, Jr., eds. Minneapolis 1972 (sites cited by number).

*Unedited Antiquities of Attica*, Society of Dilettanti. 1817.

*Untersuchungen an griechische Theatern*, H. Bulle. Munich 1928.

Valmin 1930     *Études topographiques sur la Messénie ancienne*. M. N. Valmin. Lund 1930.

Valmin 1938     *The Swedish Messenia Expedition*, M. N. Valmin. Lund 1938.

*La ville et l'Acropole d'Athènes*, Émile Burnouf. Paris 1877.

*Zeitschrift für Ethnologie*, H. Schliemann. 1884.

*Zygouries*, C. Blegen, American School of Classical Studies at Athens. Cambridge, Mass. 1928.

## Articles Cited More Than Once

*AA* 1939     "Forschungen in der Argolis," K. Gebauer, *AA* 1939, 268ff.

*AJA* 1961     "Prehistoric Habitation in Southwestern Peloponnese," W. McDonald and R. Hope Simpson, *AJA* 65, 1961, 219ff.

*AJA* 1964     "Further Exploration in Southwestern Peloponnese," W. McDonald and R. Hope Simpson, *AJA* 68, 1964, 229ff.

*AJA* 1969     "Further Explorations in Southwestern Peloponnese," W. McDonald and R. Hope Simpson, *AJA* 73, 1969, 123ff.

Åström     "Mycenaean Pottery from the Region of Aigion," P. Åström, *Op. Ath.* 5, 1964, 89ff.

*BSA* 1957     "Identifying a Mycenaean Site," R. Hope Simpson, *BSA* 52, 1957, 231ff.

*BSA* 1960     "Prehistoric Laconia Part I," Helen Waterhouse and R. Hope Simpson, *BSA* 55, 1960, 67ff.

*BSA* 1961     "Prehistoric Laconia Part II," Helen Waterhouse and R. Hope Simpson, *BSA* 56, 1961, 114ff.

*BSA* 1966     "The Seven Cities Offered by Agamemnon to Achilles," R. Hope Simpson, *BSA* 61, 1966, 113ff.

"South-western Laconia," E.S. Forster, *BSA* 10, 1903–4, 158ff.

"Gythium and the Northwest Coast of the Laconian Gulf," E.S. Forster, *BSA* 13, 1906–7, 219ff.

"Southeastern Laconia," A.J.B. Wace and F.W. Hasluck, *BSA* 14, 1907–8, 161ff.

"East-central Laconia," A.J.B. Wace and F.W. Hasluck, *BSA* 15, 1908–9, 158ff.

"Bardounia and Northeastern Maina," H.A. Ormerod, *BSA* 16, 1909–10, 62ff.

Howell     "A Survey of Eastern Arcadia in Prehistory," R. Howell, *BSA* 65, 1970, 79ff.

Sperling     "Exploration in Elis 1939," J. Sperling, *AJA* 46, 1942, 77ff.

"Notes and Inscriptions from Southwest Messenia," M. N. Tod, *JHS* 25, 1905, 32ff.

von Duhn     "Bericht über eine Reise in Achaia," F. von Duhn, *AM* 3, 1878, 60ff.

"Die Ebene von Sparta," H. von Prott, *AM* 29, 1904, 1ff.

# PLACE NAME INDEX

This index includes all place names mentioned in this book. Since these names have been taken from numerous periodicals in many languages, their spellings vary, and no attempt has been made to transliterate any specific name on a consistent basis.